# simply Cards

SALLY TRAIDMAN

10 09 08 07   5 4 3

Distributed in Canada by Fraser Direct
100 Armstrong Avenue
Georgetown, ON, Canada  L7G 5S4
Tel: (905) 877-4411

Distributed in the U.K. and Europe by David & Charles
Brunel House, Newton Abbot, Devon, TQ12 4PU, England
Tel: (+44) 1626 323200, Fax: (+44) 1626 323319
Email: mail@davidandcharles.co.uk

Distributed in Australia by Capricorn Link
P.O. Box 704, S. Windsor, NSW 2756 Australia
Tel: (02) 4577-3555

Library of Congress Cataloging-in-Publication Data

Traidman, Sally.
   Simply cards : over 100 stylish cards you can make in minutes /
Sally Traidman.-- 1st ed.
      p. cm.
   Includes index.
   ISBN-13: 978-1-58180-674-8 (alk. paper)
   ISBN-10: 1-58180-674-4
   1.  Greeting cards.  I. Title.
   TT872.T73 2006
   745.594'1--dc22
                    2005026127
Editor: David Oeters
Designer: Marissa Bowers
Layout Artist: Kathy Gardner
Production Coordinator: Greg Nock
Photo Stylist: Nora Martini
Photographers: Christine Polomsky, Tim Grondin,
Al Parrish and Cindy Traidman

F+W PUBLICATIONS, INC.

## METRIC CONVERSION CHART

| TO CONVERT | TO | MULTIPLY BY |
| --- | --- | --- |
| Inches | Centimeters | 2.54 |
| Centimeters | Inches | 0.4 |
| Feet | Centimeters | 30.5 |
| Centimeters | Feet | 0.03 |
| Yards | Meters | 0.9 |
| Meters | Yards | 1.1 |
| Sq. Inches | Sq. Centimeters | 6.45 |
| Sq. Centimeters | Sq. Inches | 0.16 |
| Sq. Feet | Sq. Meters | 0.09 |
| Sq. Meters | Sq. Feet | 10.8 |
| Sq. Yards | Sq. Meters | 0.8 |
| Sq. Meters | Sq. Yards | 1.2 |
| Pounds | Kilograms | 0.45 |
| Kilograms | Pounds | 2.2 |
| Ounces | Grams | 28.4 |
| Grams | Ounces | 0.04 |

## ABOUT THE AUTHOR

Sally Traidman is a freelance card and rubber stamp designer for rubber stamp and paper companies, and her designs appear frequently in magazines and books. She began her career as an art teacher, and then owned and operated a retail mail order rubber stamp company, called Mostly Hearts, for twenty years. She loves sharing her card crafting ideas and putting smiles on people's faces when they get real mail! Her current passions are knitting scarves and creating cards with impromptu pen sketches filled with watercolor washes. Her love of hearts is frequently part of her signature style.

## DEDICATION

To my husband, Mike; two sons, Adam and Brent; and our dog, Newton. They've put up with all my crafty clutter for many years and patiently listened to me say, "I'll be done in a minute."

To my *many* wonderful friends who have encouraged me to keep creating handmade cards. And to my precious granddaughter, Jasmine, and her mom, Cindy, who have caught "handmade card fever!"

## ACKNOWLEDGMENTS

Thanks to all my friends in the rubber stamp and paper industry. Their encouragement has been my inspiration for new cards and ideas, and I'm grateful to work with so many creative people.

Heartfelt thanks also to the wonderful staff at F+W who helped put this book together. They helped guide me through the new adventure that led to this book. Extra thanks to David Oeters, my editor, photographer Christine Polomsky and designer Marissa Bowers. They all played a big part in making this book such an enjoyable experience.

# Table of Contents

# Introduction

I received my first rubber stamp set when I was eight years old. I played with that set of simple shape stamps for hours. The fond memories of that first stamp set came flooding back when I began my career as a stay-at-home-Mom. On a whim, I bought a few rubber stamps and started decorating letters (back when people actually wrote letters!), cards, recipes and fabric among other things. I quickly amassed more stamps, and every new stamp tempted me to make another card. As you can guess, I'm still not done making cards.

You'll find plenty of cardmaking temptation in this book! These pages are filled with great ideas just waiting to be explored, enough to encourage and inspire stampers and crafters of all skill levels. You'll be asking yourself, ''why didn't I think of that?''
A quick guide in the beginning and a complete material list with every card will help get you started. Along the way are plenty of tips for personalizing your cards, trying something different and getting the most from your crafting time. As a bonus, every project in this book offers a second card that uses the same stamp!

You only need a handful of supplies to get started, and the rewards of delighting a family member or friend with a handmade card is well worth the time (believe me!). Gather your supplies, sit down for just a few minutes and you can have a finished card. Create with all your heart, and every card you make will be a work of art. Don't be afraid to give away your creations...you can always make more.

Sally Traidman

# Getting Started

Making fabulous handmade cards isn't difficult, I promise! It's made even easier with all the new tools and materials you can find in your local craft or scrapbook stores. Here's a list of some of the tools and materials, papers and adhesives to help get you started.

What are you waiting for? Cards are waiting to be made.

## Tools and materials

Below are some tools and materials that make crafting cards so much easier. You'll find most of them at your local craft, rubber stamp or scrapbook store. It's a good idea to keep all your supplies in a convenient place, so you can find them quickly when the urge to create finds you.

### STAMPS

Stamps come in a variety of shapes, patterns and designs. They are generally made of rubber, but you can also carve stamps out of erasers or vegetables such as potatoes, or make texture stamps from leaves and other objects. It's a good idea to use a *stamp cleaner* to remove inks from a stamp after use. It comes in a small bottle with a spray or sponge top and helps keep the colors pure on the stamp. See page 12 for more information on stamping and cleaning stamps.

### INKS

Stamping inks, usually applied from an ink pad, come in a variety of colors and types. *Standard dye inks* are used for general stamping. *Pigment inks* are used for general stamping and embossing. *Permanent inks* are used when the surface requires a waterproof ink for watercoloring or fabric stamping. *Pearlescent inks* are pigment inks that create a lustrous sheen when stamped. *Watermark inks* give a tone-on-tone look when stamped. *Embossing inks* stay wet longer for use with embossing powders. *Rainbow ink pads* have a variety of colors on a single pad.

### EMBOSSING POWDERS

Embossing powder is applied to wet ink and then melted to create a raised design. There are a variety of embossing powders available, from metallic such as gold to solid colors such as white, and fine powders that are useful for detailed projects. See page 14 for more information on using embossing powders.

### PASTEL CHALK

Pastel chalks come in a variety of colors that are usually organized in a plastic palette. They can be applied with a sponge applicator or your fingers. They add soft color to your projects.

### GOLD LEAFING PEN

With this chiseled-tip pen you can highlight or apply thick or thin metallic gold lines.

### PERMANENT MARKERS

These markers are permanent and should not be used directly on stamps, as they will permanently stain rubber. They are used to add a fine line, a design or words to your card or project.

### WATERCOLOR MARKERS

These water-based markers can be used to color directly on the rubber stamp to create specific areas of color on a single stamp. They can also be used to color images after you've stamped them. See page 15 for more information on using watercolor markers.

## COLORED PENCILS

These pencils come in a variety of colors and are used to shade and color images. Look for soft, leaded pencils rather than hard, since they are easier to color and blend with.

## WATERCOLOR PENCILS

These pencils can be used as you would regular colored pencils, or they can be used to create the look of watercolor in your project. Simply add water to a paintbrush and brush it over a surface colored with a watercolor pencil. The color will soften and blend.

## PAINTBRUSH

Paintbrushes come in a variety of sizes and qualities. Use a soft, small brush to color specific areas, or a big, wide brush to make a watercolor wash for a background.

## WATERBRUSH

A brush that is attached to a plastic barrel filled with water, but can also be filled with ink. Used for blending colors.

## SCISSORS

Good scissors are a necessity. Look for fine-tipped scissors that are sharp to the edge. A Teflon coating helps resist the stickiness of adhesives. You can also find *decorative-edge scissors* that have a shaped blade for cutting a variety of patterns in paper.

## PAPER TRIMMER

A cutting surface with an attached blade and ruled grid lines. An excellent tool for cutting straight lines.

## PAPER PUNCH

Paper punches are found in craft and scrapbook stores. They are useful for punching a variety of shapes out of paper.

## CRAFT KNIFE

This invaluable tool consists of a handle and a sharp, replaceable blade. Use the blade for cutting, and the back of the blade for making a sharp crease in paper. This is known as scoring.

## BONE FOLDER

A bone folder is a useful tool for making sharp fold lines across paper. An even swipe with the bone folder across the fold makes a crisp crease.

## HEAT GUN

This heat tool is used to melt embossing powders.

# Paper

You'll find an amazing number of papers at craft, scrapbook, rubber stamp and paper stores. You can even find easy-to-use packs of paper precut and prescored for folding into cards. Below are a few of the papers I used in this book. Why not take an inspirational browse through the papers at your local store and see where your creativity takes you?

## CARDSTOCK

This is the workhorse of stamping papers, and is a little thicker than standard paper. *Matte cardstock*, with its smooth surface, works with all inks. You can also find *glossy cardstock*, which has a shiny surface and works great with dye inks and markers. It remains shiny after stamping. Both kinds of cardstock come in various weights and colors.

## CREPE CARD

These ridged, textured notecards come from Japan. They are available in various colors and resemble crepe paper, but are thicker. The texture is difficult to stamp on, so it's best used as the base card.

## FABRIC PAPER

These papers are pieces of fabric, such as gingham, denim and velvet, that have been fused to paper. You can create your own fabric paper by ironing fabric and fusible web to paper.

## HANDMADE PAPER

Handmade paper is usually thicker, with an irregular surface incorporating a material such as flowers or straw. It adds an elegant, natural element to a card.

## ORIGAMI PAPER

This Japanese paper is usually very thin. Its beautiful patterns add an elegant touch to your cards.

## PEARLESCENT PAPER

This is a shiny, lustrous paper with a pearl finish. Certain inks will resist the surface, so permanent inks work best on this paper.

## PHOTO FRAME CARD

These precut frame cards come with an open area for a photo to peek through. They're great for Christmas cards and baby announcements.

## PRINTED PAPER

Scrapbooking has brought us a plethora of wonderful paper with preprinted designs to match any card. From ginghams, to dots, to flowers and plaids, printed paper is a delightful way to add instant color to your cards.

## TEXTURED PAPER

Textured paper has a surface texture such as corrugated, grass cloth, ribbed or other textures. It works best for the base of a card or for accents since it may be difficult to stamp on a textured surface.

## TSUMUGI PAPER

These finely textured, elegant papers from Japan are available in a wonderful array of colors. They are generally used as the base card.

## VELLUM

Vellum is a thin, translucent paper that is often printed with images or embossed with a raised design.

# Adhesives

With the right adhesive, your card is guaranteed to stay together. There's nothing worse than giving a card that's falling apart! Not to worry, listed below are a few adhesives I've found useful for my own projects. Don't hesitate to use the products you're most comfortable with for these projects.

### GLUE STICK

A good paper glue, such as a glue stick, is indispensable when creating cards. It can be used for adhering paper to paper and is repositionable until it starts drying. It dries clear with a fairly strong bond.

### GLUE DOTS

Glue dots are useful for adhering little trinkets, buttons, charms, ribbons and more to paper or other embellishments. They have more adhesive power and are usually thicker than paper glue, but they can also be used for mounting papers. Glue dots, which come on a roll, were used for many of the projects in this book. There are plenty of other glues in your local craft and scrapbook stores that can be used for embellishments so don't hesitate to use the glue you prefer.

### GLITTER GLUE

This product is a glue and glitter combined. It comes in a squeeze bottle with a fine tip. Glitter glue takes a little longer (20 to 30 minutes) to dry than most other glues.

### FOAM MOUNTING TAPE

This dimensional tape has a sticky surface on both sides and comes on a roll or in precut squares for mounting items. It is about $\frac{1}{8}$" (3mm) thick, so it gives your embellishments a lift and creates dimension on a card.

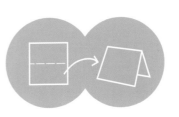

### FOLDING CARDS

The best way to fold a card is to precut the paper, then score it along the fold with the back of a craft knife. Finish creasing the fold with a bone folder. Practice folding cards or find your own method for making neat and professional-looking cards.

A standard card size is folded from an 8½" x 5½" (22cm x 14cm) piece of cardstock (known as an A2 in the paper industry) to a card that is 4¼" x 5½" (11cm x 14cm). Not all the cards in this book are that size. With every project material list in this book, you'll find the first item is the base card itself, with quick instructions on the size of the paper and how to fold it.

If folding isn't your thing, flat correspondence cards or postcards also look beautiful, or look for packs of precut and prefolded cards at your local craft store.

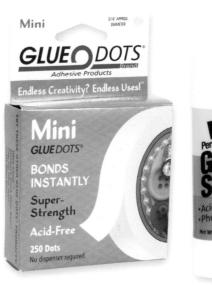

# Techniques

You might be familiar with these techniques, but I'd suggest looking them over anyway. Who knows where a new tip or idea might be hiding? The techniques on these pages also make a useful reference as you work on the projects, so don't hesitate to stop back here from time to time.

## Using Stamps

Many beautiful cards start with a great idea and a single stamp. Following these simple techniques will help prevent frustration and keep your work gorgeous.

**ONE** | When using an ink pad, ink the stamp by tapping the pad on the rubber of the stamp until the ridges of the stamp are covered in ink.

**TWO** | Press the stamp firmly on the surface you wish to stamp. Do not rock or move the stamp as you press.

**THREE** | In one smooth motion, lift the stamp from the surface, revealing the image below.

### CLEANING STAMPS

Use a stamp cleaner to clean the stamp after each use to help keep your stamp color pure and clear. Dry the stamp thoroughly with a paper towel after cleaning.

### LOOKING BEYOND THE INK PAD

You can add color to your stamp using more than just ordinary stamp pads. It's easy! Methods such as these allow you to bring new effects to your cards:

✤ Color directly on the stamp with watercolor markers. This allows you to use more than one color on a single stamp. Just work quickly to keep the ink from drying.

✤ Dab watercolors or acrylic paints on your stamp with sponges or brushes. Make sure to clean off the paint immediately after stamping, as dried paint can destroy the rubber.

# Using Masks

Masking allows you to manipulate your stamping to create depth in your images. Yellow sticky notes, which have a gentle adhesive on them for easy removal, are excellent for masks. Below are two methods of masking. Experiment and come up with your own "wow!" effects.

## MASKING THE STAMP

**ONE** | Place the mask directly on the rubber stamp, covering the area of the image you don't want to stamp. Ink the area of the image you want to stamp.

**TWO** | Remove the mask and stamp the image. Only the area you inked should appear. This will create a partial image from a larger stamp.

## MASKING THE SURFACE

**ONE** | Stamp the image you want to mask on a separate scrap of paper. Trim around the image, staying just inside the stamped lines. If desired, trim only the area that will be stamped over with the new image.

**TWO** | Place the mask over the original image on the card. Line up the mask over the stamped image. Stamp the new image over the mask and on the card surface.

**THREE** | When you remove the mask, the new stamped image should appear to have been stamped behind the original image. Used this way, masking gives the illusion of depth to your stamping.

13

# Using Embossing Powders

Embossing adds a wonderful dimensional effect to your stamped images, and it's so easy to do! It might seem intimidating at first, but once you give it a shot you'll be looking for ways to add embossed elements to all your stamping projects.

EMBOSSING

**ONE** | Ink the stamp and stamp the image to be embossed on the surface. Slow-drying embossing inks and pigment inks stay wet longer, making them especially useful for embossing.

**TWO** | While the ink is still wet from stamping, pour embossing powder over the stamped image. Tap excess powder away from the image. Save the excess powder for future projects.

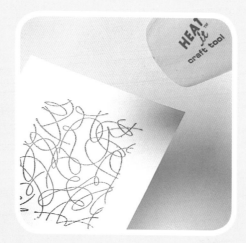

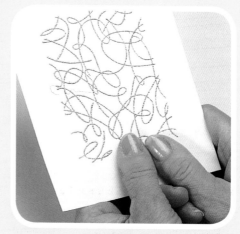

**THREE** | Heat the powder until it melts and becomes shiny. Powders melt at temperatures between 200°F-300°F (93°C-149°C). A heat gun works best, but you can also use the heat from a light bulb, iron or toaster oven to melt embossing powder.

**FOUR** | Let the powder cool before continuing unless directed otherwise in the project instructions.

# Using Watercolors

There is something special about watercolors. As you work, the positively translucent colors blend and move across the paper. Each watercolor you create is a work of art that is uniquely yours. There are few gifts as special as a handmade card decorated with gorgeous watercolors.

And you'll be amazed at how easy it is to work with watercolor. Give it a whirl!

### PAINTING WITH WATERCOLOR PENCILS

**ONE** | Color the image on the card with watercolor pencils. For the first layer, color lightly. You can always add more color and create highlights later.

**TWO** | Using a moist paintbrush, paint over the pencil marks. Be careful about how much water you use. Too much water and the colors will turn muddy. Too little and the colors won't blend at all. When you're happy with the results, let the card dry. If you feel it is necessary, add more color with the pencils and repeat this step.

### PAINTING WITH WATERCOLOR MARKERS

**ONE** | Brush the ink from watercolor markers in a palette, using a different color well for each color. Add a little water to the ink in the color well.

**TWO** | Using a brush, paint the wet ink from the palette onto the card, allowing the colors to blend on the image. If the ink begins drying in the palette, moisten with water and continue. Make sure to clean the brush thoroughly between colors.

---

**WATERCOLOR SECRETS**

Paper specifically created for watercolors works best for these watercolor techniques. Ordinary papers may wrinkle with too much water.

If you use a graphic stamp with large areas of rubber, try brushing the watercolor directly on the stamp and misting it with water. Your stamp will create a one-of-a-kind watercolor look!

# Thinking of You CARDS

Our life is filled with opportunities to make someone a handmade card. Cards are a lasting and memorable way to show friends and family you care, but all too often we let those opportunities slip by. What's stopping you from making one today?

How many times do you need to write a note to a neighbor, teacher, colleague or friend? Don't even **THINK** about using a scrap of notebook paper! Make a quick card that shows the recipient you care. Send your friends good wishes or let them know you're thinking of them with a gorgeous handmade card. Why not make a friendship card for no reason at all and just surprise someone?

While you're at it, make a few cards with the same design and tuck them away for a day you don't have time to make an entirely new card. Store them in a little card file with dividers. A notebook with acetate pockets or a box with header tabs will keep your cards organized. When you need a quick greeting, find one in your card file and personalize it before you send it off.

What are we waiting for? Time is wasting, so let's start making some of these cute, whimsical friendship cards.

**Materials** ◂ 8½" × 5½" (22cm × 14cm) Red cardstock folded to a 4¼" × 5½" (11cm × 14cm) card ▸ 2⅜" × 3½" (6cm × 9cm) Glossy white cardstock ▸ Green cardstock ▸ Cherry stamp (HOT POTATOES) ▸ Gingham stamp (HERO ARTS) ▸ Red ink ▸ Red and dark red watercolor markers ▸ Green and dark green watercolor markers ▸ 6½" (17cm) Dark green seam binding ribbon ▸ Pink and red embroidery floss ▸ Two small red buttons ▸ Glue stick ▸ Glue dots ▸ Scissors

nking of you cards thinking of you cardsthinking of you cards thinking of you cards thinking
rds thinking of you cards thinking of you cards thinking of you cards thinking of you cards th
nking of you cards thinking of you cards thinking of you cards thinking of you cards thinking
rds thinking of you cards thinking of you cards thinking of you cards thinking of you cards th
nking of you cards thinking of you cards thinking of you cards thinking of you cards thinking

# Cherries

LIFE IS A BOWL OF cherries! This sweet little card, with its pair of cherries and button embellishments, is perfect for sending fond wishes to a good friend. Personalize the card with a message inside.

**INSPIRATION CORNER**

*Make another cheery cherry card by stamping the cherries and gluing on a printed gingham ribbon tied with gold cording. Scallop the edges with scissors and glue green paper inside. You'll definitely have a friend forever when someone receives this!*

18

## STEP INSTRUCTION

**ONE** | Color directly on the stamp, using red watercolor markers for the cherries and green for the stems. Color a darker red and green around the edges to give the cherries and stems depth. Work quickly so the ink doesn't dry on the stamp.

**TWO** | Stamp the cherries on the glossy cardstock. If you're not satisfied with the results, finish coloring the cherries with the markers.

**THREE** | Stamp a line of gingham below the cherries on the glossy paper using the red ink.

**FOUR** | Thread the pink and red embroidery floss in the buttons and tie it in a knot. Trim the thread.

**FIVE** | Glue the buttons over the cherries with glue dots. Glue the glossy cardstock on the green cardstock using a glue stick. Trim the green to create a $^{1}/_{8}$" (3mm) border around the glossy cardstock. Glue the green to the center front of the red card. Tie a knot in the green ribbon and use a glue dot to glue it above the cherries. Trim the ribbon if necessary.

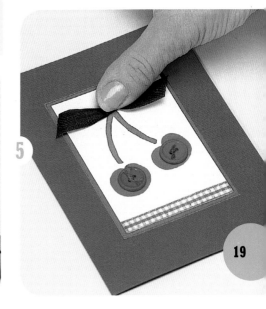

*Try this!*

Why not use a real gingham ribbon instead of the gingham stamp?

19

**Materials** ◄ 8½" × 5½" (22cm × 14cm) Sage green cardstock folded to a 4¼" × 5½" (11cm × 14cm) card ▸ Ivory cardstock ▸ Yellow cardstock ▸ Pale pink cardstock ▸ Mauve cardstock ▸ Heart bloom stamp (MOSTLY HEARTS) ▸ Flower pot stamp (MOSTLY HEARTS) ▸ Black permanent ink ▸ Orange ink ▸ Magenta watercolor marker ▸ 2" (5cm) Green satin ribbon ▸ Glue stick ▸ Glue dots ▸ Foam mounting tape ▸ Scissors ▸ Paintbrush ▸ Palette ▸ Water

# Bloomin' Heart

THIS BLOOMIN' HEART IS PERFECT for almost any occasion. Invitations, thank-you's, greetings and more, this card won't fail to please! Jot a few heartfelt words inside the card to bring the heart to full bloom.

INSPIRATION CORNER

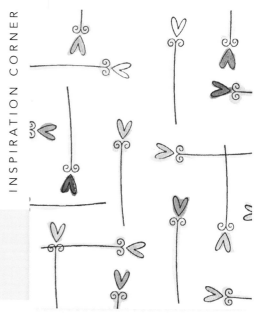

*Another easy way to use the heart bloom stamp is to stamp it in permanent black ink in all directions on the card. Add random color to the hearts with pastel chalk or watercolors.*

## STEP INSTRUCTION

**ONE** | Stamp the heart bloom on a piece of ivory cardstock using black ink. Use the magenta watercolor marker, a palette, water and a paintbrush to color the heart (see page 15 for more information on using watercolors). Trim the stamped ivory cardstock to approximately ¾" × 2" (2cm × 5cm).

**TWO** | Stamp the flower pot with orange ink on yellow cardstock and cut it out with scissors, leaving a ⅛" (3mm) border around the flower pot.

**THREE** | Glue the stamped ivory strip on the pale pink cardstock using a glue stick, trimming the pink to create a ⅛" (3mm) border around the ivory cardstock. Glue the pink cardstock to the mauve cardstock, trimming the mauve to create a ⅛" (3mm) border. Glue the mauve to the center of the sage green card, then mount the flower pot below the heart bloom using foam mounting tape.

**FOUR** | Tie a knot in the center of the green satin ribbon, then use a glue dot to secure the ribbon to the heart bloom. Trim the ribbon.

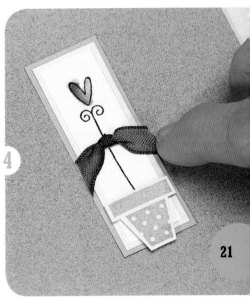

*Try this!*

Give the card some glitz by gluing a sparkling rhinestone on the heart.

21

nking of you cards thinking of you cards thinking of you cards thinking of you cards thinking
ds thinking of you cards thinking of you cards thinking of you cards thinking of you cards
nking of you cards thinking of you cards thinking of you cards thinking of you cards thinking
ds thinking of you cards thinking of you cards thinking of you cards thinking of you cards
nking of you cards thinking of you cards thinking of you cards thinking of you cards thinking

## Materials ◂ 10" × 5" (25cm × 13cm)
Oatmeal textured cardstock top-folded to a 5" (13cm) square card ▸ 2¼" (6cm) Square white cardstock ▸ Mulberry cardstock ▸ Dotted circle stamp (MOSTLY HEARTS) ▸ Dot stamp (HERO ARTS) ▸ Alphabet stamps (HERO ARTS) ▸ Small flower stamp (MOSTLY HEARTS) ▸ Green ink ▸ Black ink ▸ Three different shades of purple ink ▸ Glue stick ▸ Pencil and eraser ▸ Ruler

# Monogrammed For You

MONOGRAMMED CARDS ARE ALWAYS a stylish gift for friends and family. A card as colorful and classy as this leaves no doubt who it's from, and a wreath of hand-stamped flowers means no two cards are alike. Why not make a handful of these for a friend? They'll be perfect for a hostess gift.

INSPIRATION CORNER

22

*Use this same versatile flower stamp to create a cluster of flowers. Place a stamped flower pot below the flowers, adhering it with mounting tape. Glue a ribbon or bow on the flower pot and mount it on a piece of pre-embossed dotted paper.*

## STEP INSTRUCTION

**ONE** | Use a pencil and ruler to lightly draw a 1½" (4cm) circle on the white cardstock. Ink the dotted circle stamp with green ink. Stamp once on a piece of scrap paper, then stamp a second time in the center of the circle on the white cardstock. This second stamp should be lightly inked, leaving a pale impression.

**TWO** | Lightly stamp flowers in three different shades of purple on the pencil circle around the dotted green circle. Randomly stamp the flowers, interspersing a green dot stamp among them. Erase any remaining pencil marks after the ink dries.

**THREE** | Use black ink and a letter stamp to stamp an initial in the center of the flowers and the green circle stamp.

**FOUR** | Using a glue stick, glue the white cardstock with the stamped letter to the mulberry cardstock, trimming the mulberry to create a ⅛" (3mm) border around the white cardstock. Glue this to the center of the oatmeal card.

*Try this!*

Add texture by gluing paper or artificial flowers to the stamped flowers.

Materials◄ 7" x 7" (18cm × 18cm) White cardstock square folded to a 3½" × 7" (9cm × 18cm) card ▸White paper or watercolor paper ▸Black paper ▸Text stamp (STAMPENDOUS) ▸Black permanent ink ▸Black ink pen ▸Watercolor pencils ▸Embroidery floss (in a variety of colors) ▸Four buttons (brightly colored) ▸Glue stick ▸Glue dots ▸Scissors ▸Heart punch ▸Paintbrush ▸Water

# Hearts & Buttons

THIS COLORFUL CARD, adorned with hearts and buttons, is a celebration of friendship. Buttons, floss, punched hearts and gorgeous watercolor make this a card waiting to be treasured forever. Just like a good friend.

INSPIRATION CORNER

*Vintage paper ephemera make very appealing cards! Simply stamp the text stamp onto antique-looking paper and mount the ribboned tag onto another stamped paper. Add a twill tape message for a beautiful card you made in no time at all.*

## STEP INSTRUCTION

**ONE** | Stamp the text using black permanent ink on white paper. When the ink dries, randomly color areas of the stamp with watercolor pencils, then blend the colors using a paintbrush and water (see page 15 for information on using watercolors).

**TWO** | When dry, carefully tear the edges of the stamped white paper, leaving an area that is approximately 5" × 2½" (13cm × 6cm). Center this on the front of the white card and glue it in place.

**THREE** | Tie and knot the floss to the buttons. Trim, leaving short ends on the floss.

**FOUR** | Punch out four hearts from the black paper. Mount the hearts in a vertical line on the text using glue dots. Using a glue dot, glue a button in a random position on each heart. Use a black ink pen to make a border of dots around the torn edges of the white paper.

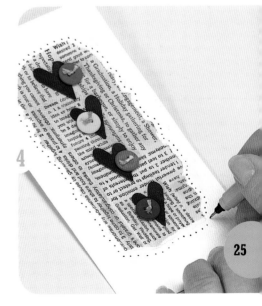

Make sure the watercolor is dry before mounting the paper to the card. If the white paper rumples, then press it between two heavy books to flatten it, or use a paper designed for watercolor projects.

**Materials** ◀ 8½" × 5½" (22cm ¾ × 14cm) Yellow cardstock folded to a 4¼" × 5½" (11cm × 14cm) card ▸ 4¼" × 2¾" (11cm × 7cm) White cardstock ▸ Green cardstock ▸ Scrap of white cardstock ▸ Narrow rectangle solid shadow stamp (HERO ARTS) ▸ Flower with stem stamps (HERO ARTS) ▸ Yellow and green ink ▸ Black permanent ink ▸ Watercolor pencils ▸ Glue stick ▸ Foam mounting tape ▸ Scissors ▸ Paintbrush ▸ Water

thinking of you cards thinking of you cards thinking of you cards thinking of you cards thinking of you cards thinking of you cards thinking of you cards thinking of you cards thinking of you cards thinking of you cards thinking of you cards thinking of you cards thinking of you cards thinking of you cards thinking of you cards thinking of you cards thinking of you cards thinking of you cards

# Friendship Flowers

RECEIVING THIS BEAUTIFUL CARD is almost as delightful as receiving a real flower delivery. Give this card as a quick pick-me-up to let friends know you're thinking of them.

INSPIRATION CORNER

*Tulips are always perky, just like this quick card! Simply use permanent black ink to stamp three flowers onto a pale pink card. Color with a light wash of watercolor, then make a flower pot out of corrugated paper and rickrack.*

26

## STEP INSTRUCTION

**ONE** | Stamp a background on the white cardstock using the shadow stamp and green and yellow ink. Try to leave a few areas of white background, but make sure your stamps are random and the areas of color irregular.

**TWO** | Stamp flowers across the background using black permanent ink. Stamp them in a row, but at various heights.

**THREE** | Stamp additional flowers on a scrap of white cardstock using the black permanent ink. Color the flowers using watercolor pencils in a variety of colors. Use a paintbrush and water to blend the colors (see page 15 for more information on using watercolors). When dry, cut out the flowers and adhere them to the top of the stamped flower stems using foam mounting tape.

**FOUR** | Glue the cardstock with flowers on green cardstock using a glue stick. Trim the green to create a ⅛" (3mm) border around the white. Glue this horizontally in the center of the yellow card.

### Tip

When making a series of stamps, such as flowers, start in the middle. This will help keep spacing even and create a more balanced feel to the card.

**Materials** 8½" × 5½" (22cm × 14cm) Sage green cardstock folded to a 4¼" × 5½" (11cm × 14cm) card ▸ 2¾" × 4" (7cm × 10cm) Green stripe printed paper ▸ Dark beige linen fabric paper ▸ Yellow cardstock ▸ Diamond pattern stamp (HERO ARTS) ▸ Daisy flower stamp (IMPRESS) ▸ Sea grass ink ▸ Soft sage ink ▸ Embossing ink ▸ White embossing powder ▸ "Thank You" twill tape ▸ Two yellow buttons ▸ Glue stick ▸ Glue dots ▸ Foam mounting tape ▸ Heat gun ▸ Scissors

# Thank-You Daisies

WHAT THANK-YOU WOULDN'T be made sweeter with a few well-placed daisies? This pretty white daisy card is perfect as a note of thanks. Be prepared for the warm welcome that's sure to follow.

INSPIRATION CORNER

28

*Photo frame cards aren't just for photos! Use a pre-cut yellow frame card and mount an embossed daisy inside the frame. Glue a small piece of pink paper behind the frame. Add opalescent sequins for shimmer.*

## STEP INSTRUCTION

**ONE** | Stamp a diamond pattern background across the sage green card using the sea grass ink. Let the ink dry.

**TWO** | Stamp the diamond pattern background on the green striped paper using a soft sage ink. Glue the striped paper on a piece of dark beige linen paper using a glue stick. Trim the linen paper to create a ⅛" (3mm) border around the striped paper.

**THREE** | On the yellow cardstock, stamp the daisy three times with embossing ink and emboss the daisies using white embossing powder (see page 14 for more information on embossing). Cut out the daisies, leaving an edge of yellow around each one.

**FOUR** | Assemble the card. Start by gluing the dark beige linen paper to the center front of the card. Mount the daisies on the green striped paper using mounting tape. Place the top and bottom daisy on the left side, and the middle on the right side. Use a glue dot to secure a button to the center of the top and bottom daisy, then glue the twill tape thank-you message on the middle daisy.

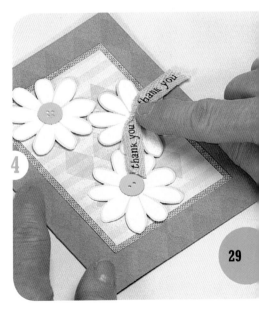

*Try this!*

You can create a personalized twill tape message using permanent ink and alphabet stamps on blank twill tape.

29

nking of you cards thinking of you cards thinking of you cards thinking of you cards thinking
'ds thinking of you cards thinking of you cards thinking of you cards thinking of you cards th
nking of you cards thinking of you cards thinking of you cards thinking of you cards thinking
'ds thinking of you cards thinking of you cards thinking of you cards thinking of you cards th
nking of you cards thinking of you cards thinking of you cards thinking of you cards thinking

# Tropical Flower Collage

THIS CARD IS ANYTHING but ordinary. By using grass cloth and origami paper, this card feels tropical and exotic. Add a simple message and it becomes appropriate for almost any occasion. Who wouldn't enjoy a taste of the exotic in their life?

INSPIRATION CORNER

30

*Recycle old paint chips and use them on your cards. This flower was stamped with pink ink, cut out and highlighted in the center with yellow chalk. Punch two holes in the middle and tie a yellow gingham ribbon on the flower for pizzazz. Mount the flower on a crackled paint chip, then glue this onto printed pink paper and trim. Adhere the pink paper on a natural looking bamboo-like card.*

## STEP INSTRUCTION

**ONE** | Stamp the flower on a scrap of white cardstock using lavender ink. Cut out the flower, leaving a border around the edges.

**TWO** | Freehand cut petal and leaf shapes from green tissue paper, origami paper and cardstock scraps. You can even use previously stamped scraps of paper.

**THREE** | Lay the petals and leaves beneath the flower, then loop various fibers over the flower and petals and secure with purple staples.

**FOUR** | Glue the looped cord vertically along the left side of the grass paper, ½" (13mm) from the edge of the paper, using glue dots.

**FIVE** | Using a glue stick, glue the grass cloth paper centered on the purple card, leaving a ¼" (6mm) purple border around the grass cloth paper. Attach the flower to the top of the card with mounting tape.

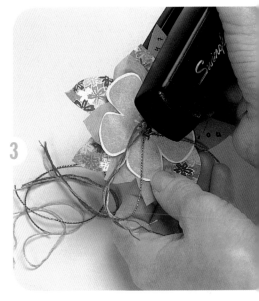

*Tip*

You can often find grass cloth paper in old wallpaper books. Search local stores for these books. Many stores will let you have them for little or no cost.

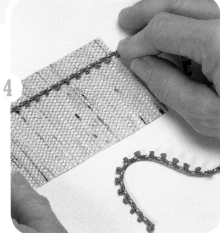

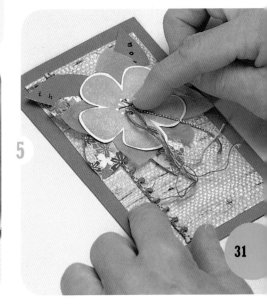

31

**Materials** ◀ 5½" × 11" (14cm × 28cm) White cardstock folded to a 5½" (14cm) square card ▸ 5" (13cm) Square starred vellum paper ▸ 4" (10cm) Square black ribbed fabric paper ▸ White cardstock ▸ Star stamp (HERO ARTS) ▸ Gold and silver ink ▸ 18" (46cm) Silver cord ▸ Glue dots ▸ Glue stick ▸ Scissors ▸ Hole punch

# You're the Star

WHY NOT MAKE SOMEONE feel like a star with this card that calls for a celebration! Place the string of stars and a gift certificate or message inside the folded vellum pocket. A little pull on the silver cord and the surprise will come tumbling out.

INSPIRATION CORNER

32

*Make another starry version of this card by adding punched star shapes. Use a thicker cardstock, or glue several of the punched stars together. Assemble a background of printed or stamped papers collaged on a white card. Anchor a piece of silver cord by adhering the stars over it with mounting tape. Glue beads and rhinestones in the center of a few stars for extra dazzle.*

## STEP INSTRUCTION

**ONE** | Place the square of vellum on your work surface so it appears diamond shaped. Fold the bottom corner up to the top corner to make a triangle. Fold the two lower corners in so they touch the opposite side, then crease.

**TWO** | Roll the front paper at the top of the triangle down, creasing each roll. Continue rolling the front paper down and into itself to create a lip of vellum for the pouch. Secure the rolled vellum against the outer paper with a glue dot. The space between the lip and the back layer of vellum is the pouch.

**THREE** | Stamp silver and gold stars on a piece of white cardstock. Cut out the stars, leaving a border around each. Cut as many stars as you would like to place on the silver cord.

**FOUR** | Punch a hole in the center of each star and string the stars on the silver cord. Tie a knot on both sides of each star to hold it in place. If you want, attach a gift certificate or message to one end of the cord.

**FIVE** | Glue the vellum pocket to the center of the black ribbed fabric paper square using a glue dot. Glue the black paper to the center of the card using a glue stick. Place the cord with the stars (and certificate or message if you added one) in the pocket, leaving the other end of the cord outside the pocket.

*Try this!*
Save time by using star confetti rather than stamped stars.

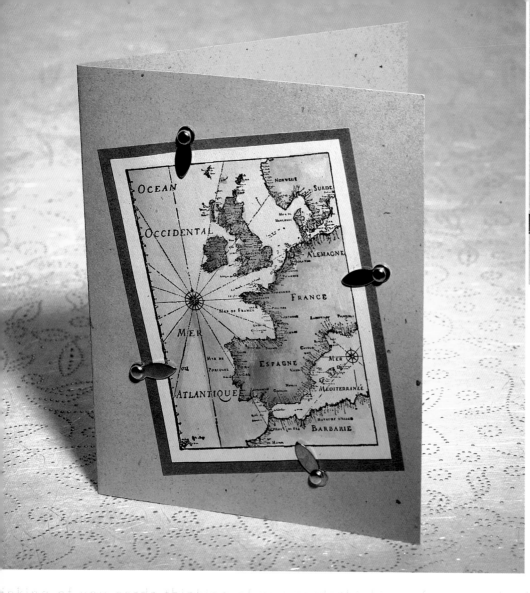

inking of you cards thinking of you cardsthinking of you cards thinking of you cards thinking
rds thinking of you cards thinking of you cards thinking of you cards thinking of you cards th
inking of you cards thinking of you cardsthinking of you cards thinking of you cards thinking
rds thinking of you cards thinking of you cardsthinking of you cards thinking of you cards th
inking of you cards thinking of you cardsthinking of you cards thinking of you cards thinking

**Materials** ◂ 8½" × 5½" (22cm × 14cm) Speckled beige cardstock folded to a 4¼" × 5½" (11cm × 14cm) card ▸ Dusty blue cardstock ▸ Tan cardstock ▸ Map stamp (HERO ARTS) ▸ Black permanent ink ▸ Watercolor pencils ▸ Frame turns ▸ Gold brads ▸ Glue stick ▸ Scissors ▸ Paintbrush ▸ Water

# Destination: Adventure

HIGH ADVENTURE LIES AHEAD! Looking for a card that's completely out-of-the-ordinary, perfect for a travel buff, a bon voyage or an adventurous friend? This map card will certainly point you in the right direction.

INSPIRATION CORNER

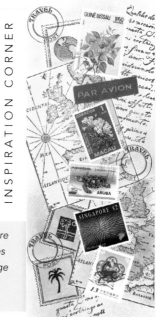

34

*Calling all used postage stamps! These little works of art are perfect for this card. First, stamp travel and postage images on a tall card. Add soft color with chalks. "Sprinkle" postage stamps across the card, adhering them with a glue stick. Voila! You're good to go.*

## STEP INSTRUCTION

**ONE** | Stamp the map with black permanent ink on the tan card-stock. Let the ink dry thoroughly. Color sections of the map with watercolor pencils, then use a paintbrush and water to blend the colors (see page 15 for information on using watercolors).

**TWO** | Trim the tan cardstock around the map, leaving a ¼" (6mm) border. Glue the tan cardstock with the map on the dusty blue cardstock with a glue stick. Trim the dusty blue cardstock to create a ¼" (6mm) border around the tan cardstock.

**THREE** | Use the frame turns and brads to attach the map to the speckled beige card. Push the brad through the hole in the frame turn, then through the card, securing the brad inside the card. Use the frame turns to hold the map in place, one on each side. Position the map on the card before securing it, slanting it across the front.

*Try this!*

Mount the map on colored cardstock that complements the colors in the map. This will make the card much more exciting and pull all the elements together.

Materials ◄ 8½" × 5½" (22cm × 14cm) White cardstock folded to a 4¼" × 5½" (11cm × 14cm) card ‣ Shadow stamp (HERO ARTS) ‣ Various cat stamps (HANKO DESIGNS) ‣ Small geometric shape stamps (HERO ARTS, MOSTLY HEARTS) ‣ Lilac, rose, vanilla and sage shadow ink ‣ Black ink ‣ Masking paper ‣ Scissors

# Cats, Cats, Cats...

THIS COLLAGE OF CATS IS purr-fect for any cat lover. Shadow inks and geometric shapes give it a retro feel. How many of us don't know someone who isn't happiest with a cat purring on her lap?

INSPIRATION CORNER

36

*This card's the cat's meow! A quick stamp and you're done. Stamp the kitty in black on a decorative (or pre-stamped) paper. Draw a horizon line through the middle of the cat with a pencil. Trim along the line and the upper half of the cat. Glue the cat stamped decorative paper onto purple and pink paper, then on a base card.*

## STEP INSTRUCTION

**ONE** │ Leave a rectangular area of the white card (an area large enough for the cat stamp) open, while masking off the rest of the card (see page 13 for information on other types of masking). Use a shadow stamp and vanilla ink to stamp the open, rectangular area. When that ink dries, move the mask and open up another area large enough for the cat stamp while masking off the rest of the card. Stamp the new open area with the shadow stamp and another color of shadow ink.

**TWO** │ Continue stamping a background for the front of the card using the shadow stamp and various inks while blocking off the rectangular areas. When you're satisfied with the background and the ink has dried, stamp the cats in black ink inside the blocks of color. Let some of the cats run off the edges of the card.

**THREE** │ Add small geometric shape stamps along the edges of the colored rectangles using the same colored shadow ink as the rectangle. These shapes will appear darker than the background.

If you don't have a shadow stamp, use a sponge to add light colors to the rectangles you block off. And for the small geometric shapes, remember that a pencil eraser can always be used for a tiny circle stamp!

**Materials** ‹ 6" × 6" (15cm × 15cm) Sour apple cardstock folded to a 3" × 6" (8cm × 15cm) card › 2¾" × 5¾" (7cm × 15cm) Printed decorative plaid paper › 1¾" × 4⅞" (4cm × 12cm) Ivory cardstock › Geometric shape stamps (HERO ARTS) › Flower stem stamp (HERO ARTS) › Turquoise, yellow, pink, lilac and green ink › Decorative sequin flowers › Glue stick › Glue dots

thinking of you cards thinking of you cards thinking of you cards thinking of you cards thinking of you cards thinking of you cards thinking of you cards thinking of you cards thinking of you cards thinking of you cards thinking

# *Blossoms of Good Wishes*

THIS CARD IS THE PERFECT pick-me-up or get-well wish for anyone feeling down. Full of baby flowers and springtime cheer, this pretty card can't help but make the day a little brighter.

## INSPIRATION CORNER

38

*These perky little flowers can be colored to match any printed paper. Ink the petals and stamp, then ink the stems and stamp. Use chalks or sponging to add a soft background color. Trim and glue the flowers on purple, and then on a card made from printed scrapbook paper.*

## STEP INSTRUCTION

**ONE** | Using the colored inks except green, stamp a row of four different geometric shapes evenly spaced down the center of the ivory cardstock.

**TWO** | Stamp the stems of the flowers in green ink on top of each of the geometric shapes. Stamp the stems at various angles, with the tops of the stems facing up.

**THREE** | Using the glue stick, glue the ivory cardstock centered on the printed decorative paper, then glue the printed decorative paper centered on the green card.

**FOUR** | Use a glue dot to mount a decorative sequin flower on the top of each stem.

Relax! It's easier to make your stamps slightly off center than try to stamp perfectly even rows. It gives your cards a more whimsical and carefree look.

nking of you cards thinking of you cards thinking of you cards thinking of you cards thi
ds thinking of you cards thinking of you cards thinking of you cards thinking of you car
nking of you cards thinking of you cards thinking of you cards thinking of you car
ds thinking of you cards thinking of you cards thinking of you cards thinking of you
nking of you cards thinking of you cards thinking of you cards thinking of you car
ds thinking of you cards thinking of you cards thinking of you cards thinking of you car

## Materials

◄ 6" × 6" (15cm × 15cm) Ivory cardstock folded to a 3" × 6" (8cm × 15cm) card ▸ 3" × 1½" (8cm × 4cm) Yellow-gold cardstock rectangle ▸ Dark green cardstock ▸ Yellow-gold cardstock scrap ▸ Vine stamp (HERO ARTS) ▸ Green tea ink ▸ Gold metallic paint pen ▸ Yellow embroidery floss ▸ Metallic gold button ▸ Glue stick ▸ Glue dots ▸ Vase paper punch ▸ Flower paper punch ▸ Scissors

# Sunflower

THERE IS SOMETHING CHEERFUL about gorgeous sunflowers. Why not capture this feeling and grow a few on paper? This is an excellent get well card for friend or family in need of good wishes.

INSPIRATION CORNER

*How simple, yet so sweet. This little tag card can blossom in no time. Stamp the vine across the tag. Punch out tiny pink flowers and glue them onto the vine. Punch a hole in the top of the card and knot the ribbon through the hole in the tag and the card. Secure the tag on the card with glue.*

## STEP INSTRUCTION

**ONE** | Punch out the vase from the dark green cardstock, and the flower from a scrap of yellow-gold cardstock.

**TWO** | Using the green tea ink, stamp the vine vertically up the center front of the ivory card, then stamp it diagonally across the vase.

**THREE** | Using the glue stick, glue the yellow-gold rectangle across the bottom of the stamped vine, trimming the edges even with the card if necessary. Glue the vase on the yellow-gold cardstock so it appears the vine is growing from the vase.

**FOUR** | Thread yellow embroidery floss in the gold button, then tie the floss in place and trim. Use a glue dot to attach the button to the flower, then glue the flower to the top of the vine.

**FIVE** | Use a gold metallic paint pen to add dots to the leaves of the vine on the vase.

## Try this!

Turn the punched-out vase upside down to make a fantastic giant balloon. Trim as needed to create the perfect balloon shape for your cards.

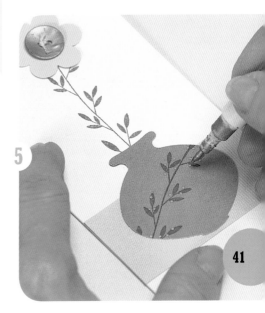

41

**Materials** ‹ 5" × 10" (13cm × 25cm) Peach Tsumugi cardstock folded to a 5" × 5" (13cm × 13cm) card › 3¼" × 3½" (8cm × 9cm) White cardstock › Black cardstock › Daisy stamp (HERO ARTS) › Woven fibers stamp (HERO ARTS) › Swirls stamp (HERO ARTS) › Writing background stamp (HERO ARTS) › Black permanent ink › Yellow, pink, lavender, peach and green pastel chalk › Glue stick › Sponge applicators › Scissors

# Sunset Daisy

RECEIVING OR SENDING A HEARTFELT card during rough times can help us all better understand the true benefits of friendship. The daisy and soft, warm pastel colors on this card make it appropriate for a sympathy card. Add a meaningful note inside to create a card that will long be cherished by the recipient.

INSPIRATION CORNER

42

*Embossing always adds an elegant touch to your cards. Stamp the woven fibers in green on a sage green cardstock. Let the ink dry, then stamp the daisy with embossing ink and sprinkle with gold embossing powder. Melt the powder and let cool. Glue the sage green cardstock to a coordinating paper and glue it to the card.*

## STEP INSTRUCTION

**ONE** | Using black permanent ink, stamp the four images on the white cardstock. Stamp the writing background on the right, the swirls in the upper left and the woven fiber in the lower left. Stamp the daisy so the stem is over the woven fiber, and the flower over the swirls. Let the ink dry.

**TWO** | Color the stamped images using pastel chalk applied with a sponge applicator. Clean the sponge regularly (see the tip below). Color each image a different color, and don't be afraid to mix the colors together with your fingers.

**THREE** | Glue the white cardstock with the stamped and chalked images onto the black cardstock. Trim the black cardstock to create a ¼" (6mm) border around the white cardstock. Center the black cardstock on the square card. When you are pleased with the position, glue it in place with the glue stick.

Tip

After using the chalk applicators several times, wash them gently with soap and water and allow them to dry. Your colors will remain pure and won't become contaminated on the card.

Materials ◂ 9" × 6" (23cm × 15cm)
Pink dot printed cardstock folded to
a 4½" × 6" (11cm × 15cm) card ▸ White
cardstock ▸ Posy stamp (HERO ARTS)
▸ Dots stamp (HERO ARTS) ▸ Stripes stamp
(HERO ARTS) ▸ Purple, bright pink and
green tea ink ▸ Green rickrack ▸ Yellow
button ▸ Fabric glue (optional) ▸ Glue
stick ▸ Glue dots ▸ Scissors ▸ Needle and
thread (optional)

# Pretty Purple Posy

EVERYONE LOVES GETTING FLOWERS. And
there's no better way to brighten someone's day
than with a flower such as this. Make this card, then
choose a friend in need of a smile. Stitching adds
a fresh and fun look to your creation.

INSPIRATION CORNER

*Bright little posies, all in a row. One, two, three, watch them grow!
Stamp the posy in three different colors and cut them out. Stamp
a green, vertical shadow stamp on a tall card. Add eyelets to the
centers of the flowers and mount them. Punch a hole in the top of
the card and tie a ribbon through it.*

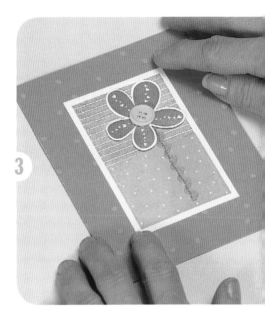

## STEP INSTRUCTION

**ONE** | Use purple ink to stamp the flower on white cardstock. Cut out the flower, leaving a tiny white border around the purple.

**TWO** | Use bright pink ink to stamp the dots on a piece of white cardstock. Use green tea ink to stamp the stripes just above the dots. Use scissors to trim the white cardstock, leaving a ¼" (6mm) white border around the stamped area.

**THREE** | Position the flower and rickrack on the stamped white cardstock. When you are satisfied with the position, stitch or glue the rickrack in place, then trim it to the desired length. Glue the flower at the top of the rickrack, then use a glue dot to glue the button in the middle of the flower. Using a glue stick, glue the white cardstock to the center front of the card.

The easiest way to line up your stamps is to start at the bottom and work your way up to the top. Peek under the stamp before you press it on the paper to line up each successive stamp.

# Moments in Time CARDS

Life is filled with special moments. Weddings, births, anniversaries and birthdays are just a few. Why not help remember and cherish those moments, as well as add to the celebration, with a handmade card?

There is something wonderful about receiving a handmade card, especially a card that celebrates those special moments. Imagine giving a birth announcement in a decorated photo frame card, with an actual photo of the newborn! How about giving a hand colored new home card to the neighbors who just moved in down the street? Or imagine creating a wedding card with gorgeous tulle and an actual ring? A handmade card helps make those moments even more special.

Honestly, now is the best time to begin making handmade cards. You can find so many great products to adorn them. Craft and scrapbook stores have loads of embellishments to jazz up a card. There's no excuse left not to start cardmaking. Find a moment in your busy day to sit down with your crafting materials, paper and glue to make a card that someone will cherish for a lifetime.

It's a great time to make a card that celebrates a special moment.

**Materials** ◄ 5¼" × 10½" (13cm × 27cm) White cardstock folded to a 5¼" (13cm) square card ▸ 4¾" (12cm) Pink cardstock square ▸ 4½" (11cm) White cardstock square ▸ 2½" (6cm) Pink cardstock square ▸ 2¼" (6cm) White cardstock square ▸ Footprints stamp (HERO ARTS) ▸ New Baby stamp (HERO ARTS) ▸ Pale pink ink ▸ Tiny clothespin embellishment ▸ Glue stick ▸ Foam mounting tape

moments in time cards moments in time cards moments in time cards moments in time cards moments in time cards moments in time cards moments in time cards moments in time cards moments in time cards moments in time cards moments in time cards moments in time cards moments in time cards moments in time cards moments in time cards moments in time cards moments in time cards moments in time cards moments in time cards moments in time cards moments in time cards moments in time cards moments in time cards moments in time cards m

# New Baby's Footprints

BEFORE YOU KNOW IT, those sweet little baby feet will be walking around in flip-flops, ballet shoes or soccer cleats. Soft little cuddly baby feet are the inspiration for this baby announcement.

INSPIRATION CORNER

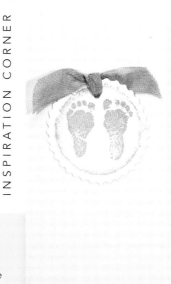

48

*Boy oh boy! You can stamp these baby feet in a heartbeat. First, lightly ink a circular stamp with blue ink. Ink heavier on the edges and stamp on white paper. Ink the feet and stamp in the center of the circle. Use decorative scissors and trim, leaving a white edge. Punch a hole and tie a ribbon in place. Mount the circle on a tall card.*

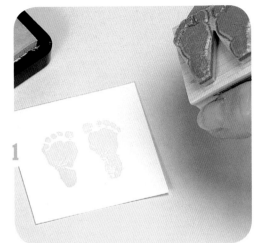

## STEP INSTRUCTION

**ONE** | Stamp the footprints in the center of the small white cardstock square using pale pink ink.

**TWO** | Stamp the words "New Baby" randomly across the larger white cardstock square using pale pink ink. Let some of the words run off the edges of the paper.

**THREE** | Glue the white cardstock with the stamped footprints to the center of the smaller pink square. Clip the top of both the smaller pink and white squares with the clothespin.

**FOUR** | Assemble the card. Glue the larger pink square in the center of the card using a glue stick. Glue the larger white square, stamped with "New Baby," in the center of the pink square. Adhere the smaller pink and white squares, both clipped with the clothespin, in the center of the card using mounting tape.

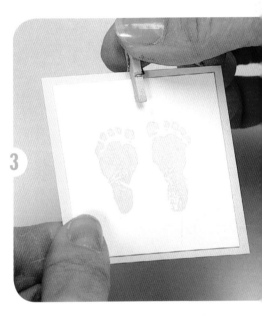

### Try this!

If you can't find the tiny clothespin embellishment, use a pretty ribbon, a bow or a tiny pink safety pin instead.

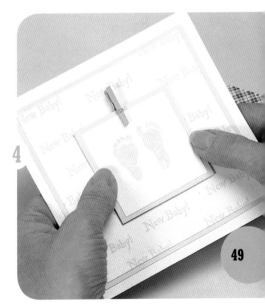

**Materials** ◀ 4¼" × 6" (11cm × 13cm) Photo frame card (can be purchased precut and folded) ▸ Pink and blue paper ▸ Paper scrap ▸ Photo (trimmed to fit the photo frame) ▸ Graphic square and graphic stripes stamps (HERO ARTS) ▸ Button stamp (MOSTLY HEARTS) ▸ Black, pale pink and pale blue ink ▸ Pink and blue embroidery floss ▸ Glue dots ▸ Foam mounting tape (optional) ▸ Scissors ▸ ¹⁄₁₆" (2mm) Hole punch

oments in time cards moments in time cards moments in time cards moments in time cards m
ts in time cards moments in time cards moments in time cards moments in time cards momen
e cards moments in time cards moments in time cards moments in time cards moments in tim
rds moments in time cards moments in time cards moments in time cards moments in time ca
oments in time cards moments in time cards moments in time cards moments in time cards m

# Precious Button Baby

THERE'S NOTHING AS PRECIOUS as a baby! Capture the moment and send a picture of your new baby or grandchild to friends and family who can't be near to celebrate the newborn.

INSPIRATION CORNER

*Create the quilted blanket background by stamping alternating pink and blue graphic squares. Use a fine-point black marker to make the stitching lines, or use a real sewing machine. Mount a printed die cut baby sticker in the center, then glue the paper on coordinating paper and glue this on the card. Simple, sweet and so cuddly soft and warm!*

50

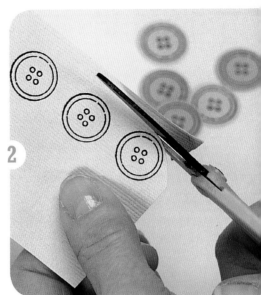

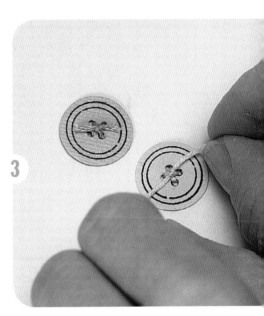

## STEP INSTRUCTION

**ONE** | Alternate using pink and blue ink to stamp graphic squares across the front of the card. Start beneath the photo frame, then stamp around the frame and the top of the card. Protect the space for the photo with a piece of scrap paper. Create a check pattern with the graphic stripe stamp. Stamp over the pink squares with pink ink, stamping both horizontally and vertically.

**TWO** | Stamp the button on scraps of pink and blue paper. Cut out three pink and two blue buttons.

**THREE** | Punch four holes in the center of each button using the hole punch. Tie embroidery floss through the holes. Secure the floss with a knot.

**FOUR** | Use glue dots or foam mounting tape to glue the buttons below the space for the photo. Use glue dots to attach the photo inside the card, so the photo can be seen through the photo frame when the card is closed.

*Try this!*

Use real buttons instead of paper buttons. It'll add an interesting element to your card, but also add to the cost of postage!

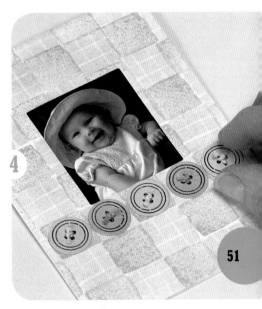

51

**Materials** ◄ 6" × 6" (15cm × 15cm) Chalk white cardstock folded to a 3" × 6" (8cm x 15cm) square ▸ 1¾" × 2⅜" (5cm × 6cm) White cardstock ▸ 2" × 2¾" (4cm × 7cm) White cardstock ▸ Pale blue and peach cardstock ▸ Baby image stamps (MOSTLY HEARTS) ▸ Chalk ink ▸ Pink chalk ▸ Fine-point black marker ▸ Embroidery floss (if desired) ▸ 3" (8cm) Silk cord ▸ Glue stick ▸ Glue dots ▸ Scissors ▸ Scallop-edged scissors ▸ Mini scallop-edged scissors ▸ 1" (3cm) Circle punch

# Bundle of Joy

NOTHING IS SWEETER THAN holding a newborn in its warm and fuzzy receiving blanket. Create your own baby blanket and tuck a precious little bundle of joy inside.

INSPIRATION CORNER

*This little tag card makes a quick baby announcement or a welcome baby card. Emboss the tiny hand with white embossing powder, then add the blue bow and a zigzag stitch with blue thread. Easily finished while baby sleeps.*

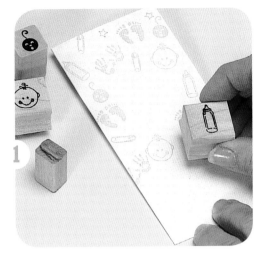

## STEP INSTRUCTION

**ONE** | Use small baby image stamps and chalk ink to randomly stamp the background on the front of the card. Fill the background as much as you can without overlapping the images.

**TWO** | Color the larger white cardstock piece with the chalk ink; there's no need to color the center of the cardstock. Trim the sides of the smaller white cardstock piece using mini scallop-edged scissors. Glue the smaller white cardstock in the center of the larger cardstock piece, framed by the chalk ink, using a glue stick.

**THREE** | Create the baby face by punching out a 1" (3cm) circle from peach cardstock. Draw the eyes and a smile with a black, fine-point marker. Use a light touch with pink chalk to add rosy cheeks. Use a glue dot to attach embroidery floss on the back of the circle for hair if desired.

**FOUR** | Freehand cut a half-circle of pale blue cardstock, 4" (10cm) wide and 2¼" (6cm) tall. Use scallop scissors to trim the outside edge. Fold the sides of the blue cardstock in so the edges touch the opposite folded sides.

**FIVE** | Assemble the card. Using a glue stick, glue the white cardstock just above the center of the card, then glue the baby blanket centered on the white cardstock. Glue the baby's head in the top of the blanket. Knot the silk cord and use a glue dot to attach it to the blanket. Trim the silk cord if necessary.

*Tip*

In a pinch, blush and eye make-up work just as well as chalk for coloring the cheeks.

53

**Materials** ◂ 8½" × 6" (22cm × 15cm) Turquoise Tsumugi cardstock folded to a 4¼" × 6" (11cm × 15cm) card ▸ 2⅞" × 3⅞" (7cm × 10cm) White cardstock ▸ Purple cardstock ▸ Stripe pattern stamp (HERO ARTS) ▸ Balloon stamp (MOSTLY HEARTS) ▸ Blue to purple rainbow ink pad ▸ Purple ink ▸ Fine-point black marker ▸ 4" (10cm) Gingham ribbon ▸ Metal "Congrats" embellishment ▸ Snap embellishment ▸ Glue stick ▸ Glue dots ▸ Scissors ▸ 1/16" (2mm) Hole punch

# Birthday Balloons

THIS BIRTHDAY CARD IS COOL, classy and festive. Don't bother giving another boring store-bought card when you can make a handmade card such as this in just a few minutes.

**INSPIRATION CORNER**

54

*Party hats always help a card or invitation look festive. Color the stripes in bright greens using markers and stamp them onto white cardstock. Trim the cardstock with tiny scallop scissors. Glue the background on a blue card. Mount a party hat sticker on the background, and add a sequin and glitter glue. Party on!*

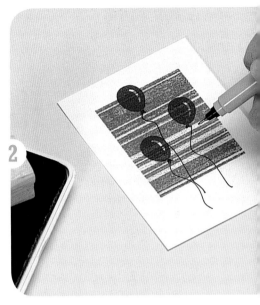

# STEP INSTRUCTION

**ONE** | Stamp the stripe pattern in the center of the white cardstock using the rainbow ink pad. Let the ink dry.

**TWO** | Stamp three balloons over the striped background using purple ink. If desired, stamp one of the images beyond the edge of the stamped background. Draw strings on the balloons with a fine-point black marker.

**THREE** | Wrap the gingham ribbon around the bottom of the white cardstock, adhering it with glue dots. Make sure the ends of the ribbon are secured on the back of the white cardstock.

**FOUR** | Assemble the card. Glue the white cardstock to a purple cardstock background using the glue stick. Trim the edges of the purple cardstock to create a ¹⁄₈" (3mm) border. Punch a tiny hole near the bottom of the stripes and adhere the metal embellishment with a snap. Glue the purple cardstock to the center of the turquoise card.

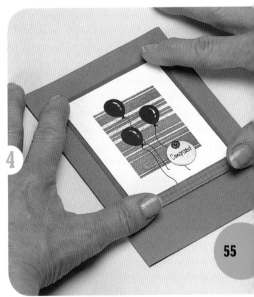

Tip

Look around your house and garage for trinkets to use on your cards. Leftover snaps from sewing, staples, eyelets, washers and more make great additions to cards.

**Materials** ◂ 6" × 6" (15cm × 15cm) Chalk white cardstock folded to a 3" × 6" (8cm × 15cm) card ▸ White cardstock ▸ Birthday cake stamp (HERO ARTS) ▸ Dot stamp (HERO ARTS) ▸ Variety of colored inks ▸ Black ink ▸ Colored markers ▸ Foam mounting tape ▸ Scissors

# Let Them Eat Cake!

A BIRTHDAY SHOULD BE a day filled with special moments. Whether you're young or old, a celebration is in order, and no birthday celebration is complete without a cake. Build this "layer" cake in a matter of minutes. Color, cut and serve!

INSPIRATION CORNER

*Dazzle someone with this bright birthday card! Stamp the cake on white paper and trim away the paper below the plate. Glue the cake on dotted paper, then color the cake with markers. Tie ribbons through a punched hole. Connect the card and ribbon with a zigzag stitch. Add glitter to the candles for extra sparkle.*

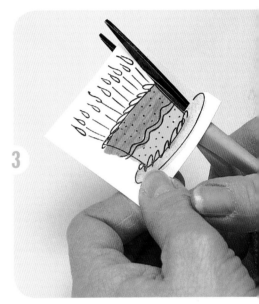

## STEP INSTRUCTION

**ONE** | Start by inking *only* the cake and candles on the birthday cake stamp using black ink. *Do not* ink the plate. Stamp the cake on the front of the card, centered about 1" (3cm) from the top.

**TWO** | On a piece of white cardstock, stamp the cake, candles and plate three times. Color the cake using a variety of colored markers. Don't worry about coloring neatly.

**THREE** | Cut out the cakes, making sure to cut off the candles. For one of the cakes, leave the plate in place. For the other two cakes, cut off the plate. Color the plate left in place using a light blue marker.

**FOUR** | Neatly color the stamped cake and candles at the top of the card using colored markers. On the card, mount the other cakes below the stamped cake using mounting tape. Layer the cakes so they touch one another, and make sure the cake with the plate is on the bottom of the card. Use the dot stamp and a variety of inks to surround the cake with colored dots.

*Try this!*

It's fun to make cards any size you want: tall and skinny, small, square or oversize. If your card isn't standard size, make your own envelope with coordinated paper.

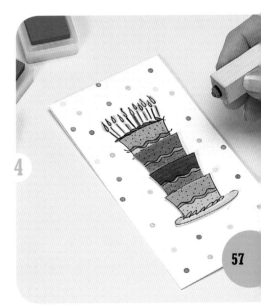

57

# Birthday Candles

GO AHEAD, MAKE A WISH and blow out the candles. Didn't work? Well, go ahead and make someone's birthday a bit more happy when you give them these festive candles on a handmade card.

INSPIRATION CORNER

This versatile brushstroke stamp can be candles, a cake, a background color and more! Stamp the brushstroke three times, in green, pink and yellow, to make a layer cake. Draw the candles and stamp yellow hearts for the flame. Glue or stitch rickrack between the layers. It's quicker than baking and has fewer calories too!

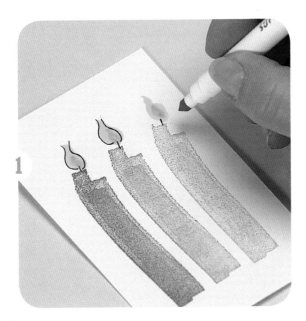

## STEP INSTRUCTION

**ONE** | Using green ink and the brushstroke stamp, stamp a "candle" in the middle of the white cardstock. Stamp a pink candle to the left and a turquoise one on the right of the original green candle. Draw flames on the candle with yellow and orange markers. Add a wick and trace around the flames with a fine-point black marker. Use colored markers to draw dots, squiggles and other designs on the candles.

**TWO** | Use the hole punch to punch holes around the edge of the turquoise paper. Create a border of holes ⅓" (8mm) wide around the turquoise paper. When finished, use a glue stick to glue the turquoise paper centered over the yellow cardstock. The yellow should show through the holes in the turquoise paper.

**THREE** | Assemble the card. Glue the punched turquoise paper in the center of the aqua card. Glue the stamped white cardstock in the center of the turquoise. Adhere the jeweled stickers in the middle of each candle flame.

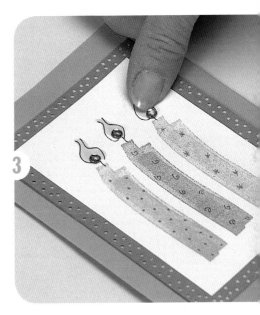

*Try this!*

Save time by using a patterned paper with yellow dots instead of punching your own pattern.

**Materials** ◀ 8½" × 6" (22cm × 15cm) Ivory crepe cardstock folded to a 4¼" × 6" (11cm x 15cm) card ▸ 3½" × 4½" (9cm × 11cm) White cardstock ▸ ¾" × 1¾" (19mm × 4cm) Ivory cardstock (cut to a tag shape) ▸ Decorative orange paper ▸ Multiple squares shadow stamp (HERO ARTS) ▸ Single square shadow stamp (HERO ARTS) ▸ Birthday image stamps (MOSTLY HEARTS) ▸ Birthday message stamp (HERO ARTS) ▸ Orange, yellow, red and pink ink ▸ Black ink ▸ 5" (13cm) Ribbon ▸ Glue stick ▸Scissors ▸ Hole punch ▸ Craft knife

moments in time cards moments in time cards moments in time cards moments in time cards moments in time cards moments in time cards moments in time cards moments in time cards moments in time cards moments in time cards moments in time cards moments in time cards moments in time cards moments in time cards moments in time cards moments in time cards moments in time cards moments in time cards moments in time cards moments in time cards moments in time cards

# Surprise!

ADD A LITTLE FUN to your birthday wishes with this card. A surprise hides in a secret pocket in the card. Shhh, don't give it away!

## INSPIRATION CORNER

60

*Presents and party hats add up to merriment and fun! Stamp these birthday images over stamped blocks of color. Add more color to the stamps with markers or colored pencils. Stitch a lavender strip to the bottom, then trim using pinking shears. Glue this to the front of an aqua card.*

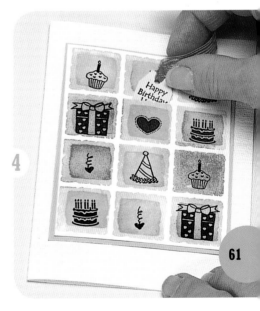

## STEP INSTRUCTION

**ONE** | Ink the multiple squares shadow stamp with a variety of colors, blending the colors together if you wish. Stamp the squares in the center of the white cardstock.

**TWO** | Add depth to the stamped squares by stamping a single square shadow stamp using a darker colored ink in each of the squares. Let the ink dry.

**THREE** | Stamp birthday images in each of the boxes using black ink. When dry, use a craft knife to cut an opening in the top of one of the boxes.

**FOUR** | Stamp a birthday message on the small piece of ivory cardstock cut to a tag shape. Punch a hole in the top of the tag and tie the ribbon through the hole, then trim the ribbon. Trim the stamped white cardstock around the stamped area, then glue it to the decorative orange paper. Glue only the edges of the white cardstock, so you don't glue the cut opening closed. Trim the orange paper to create a $1/8$" (3mm) border around the white cardstock. Glue the orange paper to the center of the card. Insert the birthday message tag inside the cut opening.

**Tip**

If you don't have a stamp with multiple squares, just use a single square stamp and stamp multiple times across the white cardstock. No problem!

**61**

## Materials◄ 8½" × 5½" (22cm × 14cm) Speckled white cardstock folded to a 4¼" × 5½" (11cm × 14cm) card

▸ 2⅛" × 3" (5cm x 8cm) Yellow cardstock

▸ 2⅛" × 3" (5cm x 8cm) Black cardstock

▸ 2" × ½" (5cm x 1cm) White vellum ▸ White cardstock ▸ Gold cardstock ▸ Metallic gold vellum ▸ Graduation hat stamp (HERO ARTS)

▸ Black ink ▸ Fine-point permanent black marker ▸ Gold leafing pen ▸ Gold cording

▸ Glue stick ▸ Foam mounting tape ▸ Glue dots ▸ Scissors ▸ Large and small star punches

moments in time cards moments in time cards moments in time cards moments in time cards moments in time cards moments in time cards moments in time cards moments in time cards moments in time cards moments in time cards moments in time cards moments in time cards moments in time cards moments in time cards moments in time cards moments in time cards moments in time cards moments in time cards moments in time cards moments in time cards moments in time cards moments in time cards moments in time cards moments in time cards moments in time cards moments in time cards moments in time cards moments in time cards moments in time cards moments in time cards moments in time cards

# *Graduation Day*

SEND THIS STELLAR CARD to a "star" graduate. Decorative paper punches, rolled vellum and gold cording add all the pizzazz the recent graduate deserves. Write a personal mesage for the graduate inside the card.

INSPIRATION CORNER

HAPPY GRADUATION

*Hats off to our graduates! Stamp these hats in the school colors and glue confetti made from tiny square paper punches across the card. Add words at the bottom. Trim the paper to fit a tall base card.*

## STEP INSTRUCTION

**ONE** | Stamp the graduation hat on white cardstock using black ink. Cut it out, making sure to cut off the stamped tassel. Tie three 3" (8cm) gold cords into a tassel. Trim the ends of the tassel as desired and use a glue dot to glue them onto the hat.

**TWO** | Punch out small stars in gold cardstock. Punch out a large gold star from gold vellum and white cardstock. Using a glue stick, glue the gold vellum star to the white cardstock for added strength.

**THREE** | Ink the edges of the large gold star with the leafing pen.

**FOUR** | Create a diploma by rolling up the small piece of white vellum. Tie the vellum closed with a small piece of gold cording. Trim the cording if necessary.

**FIVE** | Use a glue stick to glue the black cardstock on the front of the speckled white card, slanting it to the left. Glue the yellow cardstock over the black, slanting it as well. Glue the large star in the center of the yellow, and the smaller stars around it. Glue the diploma under the large star. Mount the graduation hat across the star using mounting tape. Finally, edge the yellow cardstock with dots using the fine-point black marker.

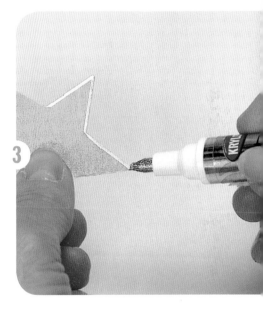

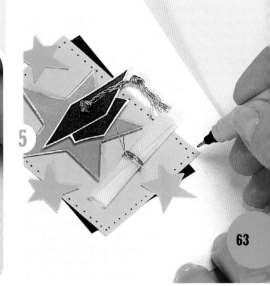

*Try this!*

Why not outline the yellow card-stock with dots, lines, zigzags or a favorite squiggle?

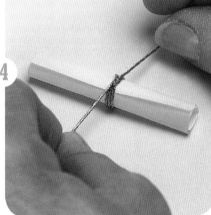

63

**Materials** ◂ 8½" × 6" (22cm × 15cm) Beige crepe cardstock folded to a 4¼" × 6" (11cm x 15cm) card ▸ 1¼" × 1½" (3cm × 4cm) Oatmeal speckled paper ▸ 2⅛" × 3½" (5cm × 9cm) White pearlescent paper ▸ Bride and groom stamp (STAMPENDOUS) ▸ Black permanent ink ▸ Gold ink ▸ Colored pencils ▸ Tiny cream envelope ▸ 6" (15cm) White tulle ▸ Two decorative gold rings ▸ Glitter glue (optional) ▸ Glue stick ▸ Glue dots ▸ Scissors

# With This Ring

SIMPLE, BUT BEAUTIFUL. So many people strive to make their wedding a simple event that will always be remembered. Let these little gold rings, which represent the circle of life, adorn this simple, but beautiful, wedding card.

INSPIRATION CORNER

64

*Cheers to the bride and groom! Ink the edges of four small shadow stamps. Stamp the bridal images inside. Let dry and add color to the images, then cut out the squares. Glue the stamped bride and groom to metallic gold paper. Scatter and glue these images across the tall card. Add flower stickers and bits of gold paper. Add beads to the flowers to finish.*

## STEP INSTRUCTION

**ONE** | Stamp the bride and groom in the center of the oatmeal paper using black ink.

**TWO** | Add color to the stamped bride and groom using colored pencils. Color the bouquet lightly using pink and green. Ink the edge of the paper using a gold ink pad. If desired, add glitter to the veil and dress with glitter glue.

**THREE** | Tie the rings together using the tulle, then trim the tulle.

**FOUR** | Assemble the card. Glue the pearlescent paper to the center front of the beige card using a glue stick. Plan the position of the envelope and the stamped oatmeal paper on the pearlescent paper. Place the envelope at an angle on the lower half of the pearlescent paper. Place the stamped oatmeal paper, also at an angle, peeking out of the envelope. When you are happy with the position, glue them both in place. Finally, use a glue dot to attach the tulle with the rings to the front of the envelope.

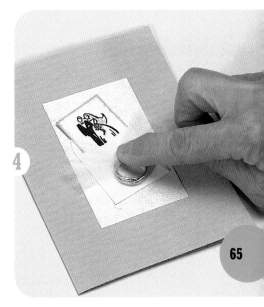

*Try this!*

If you know the bridal party colors, why not color coordinate your card and envelope to match them?

**Materials** ◂ 6" × 6" (15cm × 15cm) Chalk white cardstock folded to a 3" × 6" (8cm × 15cm) card ▸ 1½" × 2¼" (4cm × 6cm) Cornflower blue cardstock ▸ Cardstock scrap ▸ Double stripe stamp (PRINTWORKS) ▸ Small heart stamp (HERO ARTS) ▸ Square shadow stamp (HERO ARTS) ▸ Pearlescent blue ink ▸ 5" (13cm) Blue seam binding ribbon or regular ribbon ▸ Wedding cake sticker ▸ Opalescent sequins ▸ Glue stick ▸ Glue dots ▸ Foam mounting tape ▸ Scissors

oments in time cards moments in time cards moments in time cards moments in time cards m

# Eat, Drink and Be Married!

THIS CARD WON'T KEEP YOU from getting to the party on time. It's made with a sticker, so all you have to do is stamp the background and paste on the sticker. Voila!

INSPIRATION CORNER

*Use this card for more than just weddings! It would be a wonderful anniversary card, or a delightful thank-you note. Just stamp the double stripes in blue on the blue photo card. Punch out a gold heart, then trim around the empty heart space to make an outline heart. Glue the hearts inside the frame and add ribbon. Simple!*

## STEP INSTRUCTION

**ONE** | Create a background on the front of the card using pearlescent blue ink and the double stripe stamp. First stamp vertical lines across the front of the card, then stamp horizontal lines. Keep the spacing between lines as even as possible, and make sure to leave enough room between lines for the small heart stamps.

**TWO** | Stamp a heart in some of the open areas between lines using the pearlescent blue ink. Stamp randomly, making sure to leave more open spaces between lines than hearts.

**THREE** | Using the pearlescent blue ink, stamp the square shadow stamp centered near the top of the small blue piece of cardstock.

**FOUR** | Assemble the card. Wrap the 5" (13cm) blue ribbon around the blue cardstock, tying the ribbon in a knot below the shadow stamp, trimming the ribbon ends. Position the blue cardstock centered near the top of the card. Adhere the sticker to cardstock and cut it out. Mount the sticker over the shadow stamp and above the ribbon on the blue cardstock using mounting tape. When you are pleased with the position of the card elements, secure the cake sticker with mounting tape, then secure the blue cardstock with the glue stick. Finally, apply the sequins to the cake using glue dots.

*Tip*

You can also use clear nail polish instead of glue dots to secure the tiny sequins.

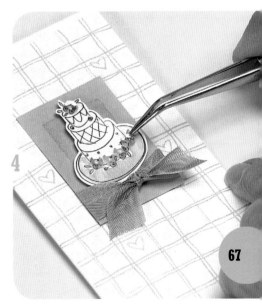

**Materials**◄ 8½" × 6" (22cm × 15cm) Beige speckled cardstock folded to a 4¼" × 6" (11cm × 15cm) card ▸3" × 1¾" (8cm × 5cm) Corrugated brown paper ▸Swirl hearts stamp (IMPRESS) ▸White pigment ink ▸Gold leafing pen ▸6" (15cm) Metallic gold thread or cording ▸Glue stick ▸Scissors ▸Heart paper punch

moments in time cards moments in time cards moments in time cards moments in time cards moments in time cards moments in time cards moments in time cards moments in time cards moments in time cards moments in time cards moments in time cards moments in time cards moments in time cards moments in time cards moments in time cards moments in time cards moments in time cards moments in time cards moments in time cards moments in time cards moments in time cards moments in time cards

# Dancing Hearts

A HEART IS A BEAUTIFUL SYMBOL. If one heart is good, how about two dancing hearts on a card? The playful hearts on this gorgeous card are perfect for a wedding or anniversary.

INSPIRATION CORNER

*This heart collage card can be made from the paper and card scraps you just couldn't throw away. Stamp the swirl hearts in white ink on beige paper. Add scraps of various papers, punch outs, ribbons and brads.*

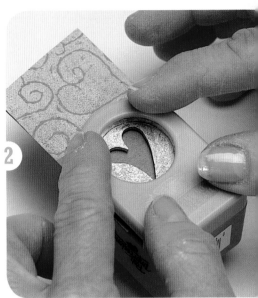

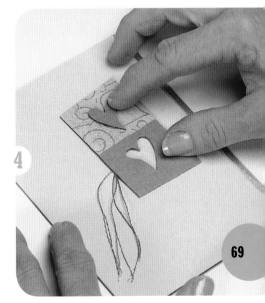

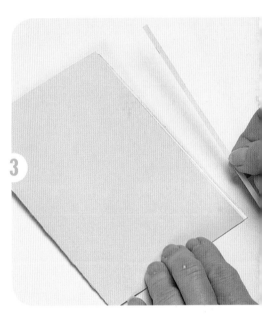

## STEP INSTRUCTION

**ONE** | Stamp the swirl hearts on the back (untextured side) of the corrugated brown paper using white ink. Leave enough room below the stamp for the heart punch. Let the ink dry.

**TWO** | Trim the sides of the corrugated brown paper evenly around the swirl hearts stamp, but trim the top with one side higher than the other. Trim the bottom, leaving enough room for a punched heart below the stamp. Punch a heart just below the stamped area. Line up the punch to make sure you've positioned the punch correctly. Save the heart to use later.

**THREE** | Create a gold leaf border on the card. Line the right edge inside the card using the gold leafing pen. Cut a ⅛" (3mm) strip from the right front edge of the card to reveal the border inside the card.

**FOUR** | Assemble the card by gluing the brown corrugated paper on the upper right side of the card front using a glue stick. Insert the looped gold thread beneath the brown paper before securing the paper. Glue the heart you punched from the corrugated brown paper on top of the stamped area.

Turn the punch upside down so you can see exactly where you'll be punching.

oments in time cards moments in time cards moments in time cards moments in time cards m
nts in time cards moments in time cards moments in time cards moments in time cards mome
e cards moments in time cards moments in time cards moments in time cards moments in tin
rds moments in time cards moments in time cards moments in time cards moments in time c.
oments in time cards moments in time cards moments in time cards moments in time cards m

**Materials** ◀ 5" × 7" (13cm × 18cm) Deckle-edged ivory card (can be purchased precut and prefolded) ▸ 3" × 4¼" (8cm × 11cm) Pearly white cardstock ▸ 1¼" × 1¾" (3cm × 4cm) Ivory cardstock ▸ Metallic gold cardstock ▸ Scribble background stamp (HERO ARTS) ▸ Metallic gold ink ▸ Gold embossing powder ▸ 10" (25cm) Gold mesh ribbon ▸ 5" (13cm) Gold mesh ribbon ▸ Small gold heart charm ▸ Glue stick ▸ Glue dots ▸ Heat gun ▸ Standard hole punch

# Heart of Gold

THIS ELEGANT GOLD EMBOSSED card would work for any anniversary, not just a golden one. After all, what can be more elegant than gold, and what symbolizes love as well as a heart? Make every anniversary a golden treasure.

INSPIRATION CORNER

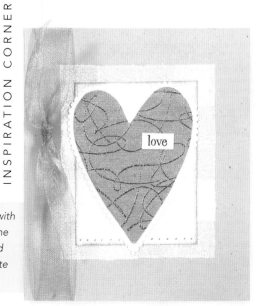

70

*Stamp and emboss a large shadow stamp in white on beige paper. Edge a white paper with gold ink and glue it on the shadow stamp, then add tiny dots with a gold pen. Emboss the scribble stamp with gold on gold paper and cut out a heart. Mount it on white paper and trim with tiny scallop scissors, then glue it on the edged paper. Stamp a message on white paper and glue it to the heart. Finally, tie a fancy gold bow around the front of the card.*

## STEP INSTRUCTION

**ONE** | Punch a series of holes on the right side of the deckle edged card. Punch the first hole ½" (13mm) from the bottom and ½" (13mm) from the right edge. Punch each hole ½" (13mm) up from the last. Inside the card, anchor the end of the 10" (25cm) gold mesh ribbon below the bottom hole with a glue dot, then weave the ribbon through the holes, going in one hole and up through the next. Anchor the other end of the ribbon with a glue dot inside the card when you finish weaving. Trim the ribbon if necessary. Note: You can make your own deckle edge card by trimming a card with deckle scissors or tearing the edge of a card against a straight edge. You may want to soften the paper with water before tearing.

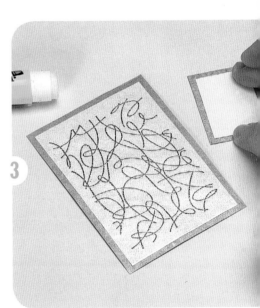

**TWO** | Stamp the scribble background with gold ink on the pearly white cardstock, then emboss it with gold powder. Melt the embossing powder with a heat gun (see page 14 for more information on embossing).

**THREE** | Glue the pearly white cardstock to a piece of metallic gold cardstock with a glue stick. Trim the gold cardstock to create a ⅛" (3mm) border around the pearly white cardstock. Glue the smaller ivory cardstock on metallic gold cardstock, trimming the gold cardstock to create a ⅛" (3mm) border around the ivory.

**FOUR** | Glue the pearly white cardstock, mounted on the gold cardstock, to the front of the card. Glue the ivory cardstock on the pearly white cardstock, positioning it just above the center of the pearly white cardstock. Thread and knot the 5" (13cm) gold ribbon through the gold heart charm. Trim the excess ribbon and use glue dots to attach the charm and ribbon to the center of the ivory cardstock.

*Tip* When using embossing powder, make sure you shake off the excess powder before you use the heat gun or you'll have specks of melted powder around your design.

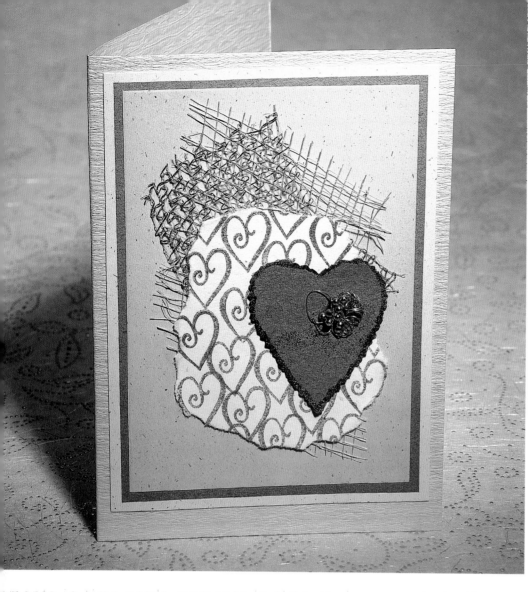

Materials ◀ 8½" × 6" (22cm × 15cm) Beige crepe cardstock folded to a 4¼" × 6" (11cm x 15cm) card ▸ 3⅜" × 4⅞" (9cm × 12cm) Beige flecked cardstock ▸ Dusty rose cardstock ▸ Ivory cardstock ▸ 4" (10cm) Square of white cardstock ▸ Heart stamp (HERO ARTS) ▸ Gold metallic ink ▸ Gold embossing powder ▸ Thin gold wire ▸ Tiny gold seed beads ▸ Loose weave straw mesh ▸ Gold mesh ribbon ▸ Glue stick ▸ Glue dots ▸ Heat gun ▸ Scissors ▸ Tweezers ▸ Thin paintbrush handle

moments in time cards moments in time cards moments in time cards moments in time cards m
ts in time cards moments in time cards moments in time cards moments in time cards moment
e cards moments in time cards moments in time cards moments in time cards moments in time
rds moments in time cards moments in time cards moments in time cards moments in time car
moment in time cards moments in time cards moments in time cards moments in time cards m

# Collage of Hearts

AS TIME PASSES, YOU realize just how many elements work together to make a successful marriage. This card is perfect for an anniversary, but it works as a Valentine's Day or a simple *I Love You* card as well.

INSPIRATION CORNER

*Find those paper scraps you've been saving and emboss various heart shapes on them. Haphazardly trim the edges to funky squares and arrange them on the front of the card. Ink and deckle the edge of the card with a gold leafing pen.*

72

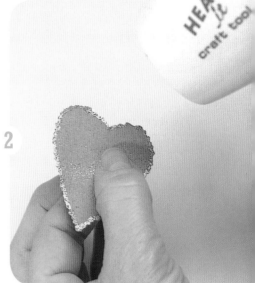

## STEP INSTRUCTION

**ONE** | Use gold ink to stamp a heart across a 4" (10cm) square of white cardstock. Fill the paper with hearts, even over the edges. When you've finished stamping and the ink is dry, tear the edges of the paper.

**TWO** | Tear or cut out a heart shape from the dusty rose cardstock. The heart shape should be about 2" (5cm) tall. Use gold ink and gold embossing powder to emboss the edges and a small area in the center of the heart (see page 14 for more information on embossing).

**THREE** | Coil the gold wire around a thin paintbrush handle. Continue until you're satisfied with the shape of the coil.

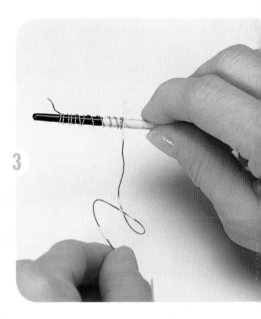

**FOUR** | Remove the coil from the paintbrush handle. Thread beads on the coiled wire using tweezers, then flatten the wire. Glue more beads on the outside of the coil using glue dots. Continue until you are satisfied, then trim the excess wire.

**FIVE** | Cut and fray the edges of a small piece of gold mesh ribbon and straw mesh. Place the straw mesh on the beige cardstock, then layer the gold ribbon over the straw. Place the white paper with gold hearts over the ribbon. Place the dusty rose heart to one side of the paper. When satisfied with the placement, use a glue stick to secure the elements. Next, use a glue dot to attach the wire embellishment over the embossed center of the heart. Glue the beige cardstock to the dusty rose cardstock, trimming the edges to create a 1/8" (3mm) border. Glue the dusty rose cardstock to ivory cardstock, trimming the edges to create a 1/8" (3mm) border. Glue the ivory cardstock to the center of the card front.

### Try this!

Be creative with your collage! Try different papers, other stamps in your collection or various embellisments. Experiment with the arrangement and design before securing the collage in place.

## Materials ◀ 7" × 6" (18cm × 15cm)

Moss green textured cardstock folded to
a 3½" × 6" (9cm x 15cm) card ▸ 2½" × 5½"
(6cm × 14cm) White cardstock
▸ Light green cardstock ▸ House stamp
(MOSTLY HEARTS) ▸ Leaf stamp (HERO ARTS)
▸ Black permanent ink ▸ Watercolor markers
▸ Glue stick ▸ Paintbrush ▸ Palette ▸ Water

# A New Home

BOXES, MOVING VANS, NEW neighbors and a
whole new life! There are few times as exciting as
moving into a new home. Stamp a new home card
in a matter of minutes. Attach it to a plate of cookies
or bottle of wine and take a moment to greet your
new neighbors.

### INSPIRATION CORNER

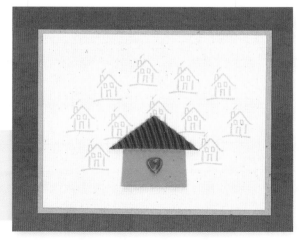

**74**

*Why not tailor the colors of the card to the colors of the new home? For this
brown house with a red roof, randomly stamp the house in tone-on-tone color
for the background. Cut a scrap of rust corrugated paper in a triangle and a
rectangle of colored cardstock for the house. Glue the house in the middle of
the background, then add a heart charm to the house. Simple!*

## STEP INSTRUCTION

**ONE** | Turn the white cardstock so it lies horizontally on your work surface. Using black permanent ink, stamp a row of houses in a zigzag line across the middle of the cardstock.

**TWO** | Ink the stamp with green markers for the leaves and brown for the trunks of the trees. Randomly stamp leaves to look like trees in the background and between the houses.

**THREE** | Paint the houses using watercolors from the watercolor markers, a paintbrush, water and a palette (see page 15 for more information on watercolors). Allow some of the color to bleed into the trees.

**FOUR** | Assemble the card. Glue the white cardstock on the light green cardstock using a glue stick. Trim the green to create a ⅛" (3mm) border around the white. Glue this to the center of the moss green card.

*Try this!*

Blend your brush markers directly on the stamp. You never know what lovely colors you'll discover.

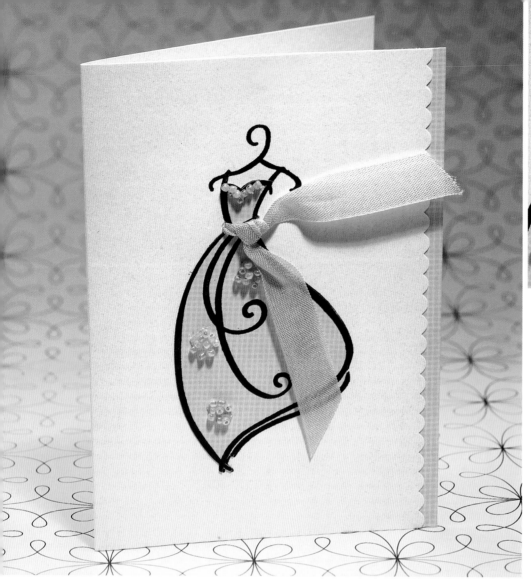

## Materials ◄ 8½" × 6" (22cm × 15cm) Speckled white cardstock folded to a 4¼" × 6" (11cm × 15cm) card

▸ Pink gingham printed paper
▸ Gown stamp (STAMPENDOUS) ▸ Black ink ▸ 7" (18cm) Pink ribbon ▸ Pink and white seed beads ▸ Glue stick ▸ Glue dots
▸ Craft knife ▸ Scissors ▸ Scallop scissors
▸ Tweezers

# Belle of the Ball

WHEN PLANNING THE SOCIAL event of the season, don't send a mediocre invitation! This pretty-in-pink card is the perfect invitation for get-togethers, special birthdays, engagements or a bridal shower.

**76**

INSPIRATION CORNER

*Make this gown into a bridal shower thank-you card by stamping it in blue ink on blue paper. Mount it on lilac paper, and then onto silky white cardstock. Attach the bow, add glitter to the bodice and opalescent sequins to the bottom of the dress.*

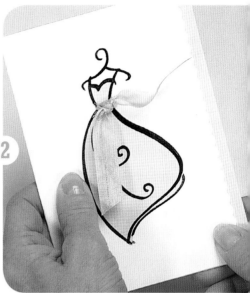

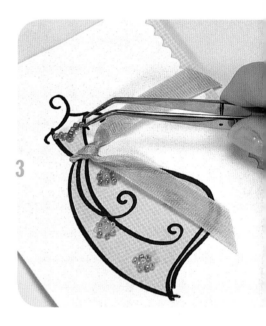

## STEP INSTRUCTION

**ONE** | Using black ink, stamp the dress in the center front of the speckled white card. Stamp the dress again on the pink gingham paper. Cut out the pink gingham dress, cutting off the hanger and straps of the dress. Using a glue stick, glue the pink gingham dress over the dress on the card. The stamped hanger and straps should extend above the pink gingham dress.

**TWO** | Make two slits through the front of the white card on either side of the waist of the dress using a craft knife. Thread the pink ribbon through the waist and knot it in the front, trimming the excess. Use scallop-edged scissors to cut a ¼" (6mm) border from the right side of the front of the card. Trim a piece of pink gingham paper so it lines the entire inside of the card (backing the scalloped edge and hiding the loops of pink ribbon). Glue it inside the card.

**THREE** | Using glue dots, glue pink and white seed beads as decorative accents on the dress. Glue a line of seed beads at the top of the dress. With a white bead as the center and pink seed beads as petals, make bead flowers on the dress.

*Try this!*

Make this card and dress all in white and add white tulle instead of ribbon for a wedding.

# Seasonal Delights CARDS

A holiday is the perfect reason to send a card (not that we really need a reason). In this section, you'll find great ideas for holiday cards such as New Year's, Valentine's Day, Easter, Thanksgiving and Christmas as well as seasonal cards. There are plenty of ideas to take you through the entire calendar year. Celebrate fall with a gorgeous autumn card, or usher in spring with a bunny card that will have people talking!

Inspiration for handmade cards doesn't wait for a season. If you have a good idea for Halloween in the spring, jot it down in a card file or sketch it out so you won't forget it. Better yet, make the card now and then tuck it away. Ideas come at all times of the day and night, so keep a pad handy so you can write down your thoughts.

You'll be so delighted with your creations, you won't be able to wait until the next holiday to make another card!

**Materials** ◄ 8½" × 6" (22cm × 15cm) Ivory crepe cardstock folded to a 4¼" × 6" (11cm × 15cm) card ▸ 3½" × 3½" (9cm × 9cm) White cardstock ▸ White cardstock scrap ▸ Purple, gold and metallic gold paper ▸ Swirls, spirals and circles stamps (HERO ARTS) ▸ Happy New Year stamp (HERO ARTS) ▸ Metallic gold, black and lime green ink ▸ Colored chalks ▸ Metallic gold thread ▸ Adhesive tape ▸ Foam mounting tape ▸ Glue stick ▸ Sponge applicators ▸ Scissors ▸ ¾" (19mm) Circle punch ▸ Star punch

# Happy New Year!

THE BIG BUBBLES AND spirals on this card resemble champagne bubbles on New Year's, and the colors are both elegant and festive! Let this card help ring in your New Year's celebration.

*Glitz up your New Year's card with some sparkling sequins and gold threads. Randomly stamp circles and spirals in a variety of colors on an irregularly shaped rectangle. Adhere the rectangle to the blue background by stitching gold "streamers" using gold thread and opalescent sequins. Mount a cut-out swirl over the streamers. Add lettering and the date.*

INSPIRATION CORNER

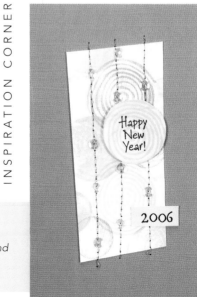

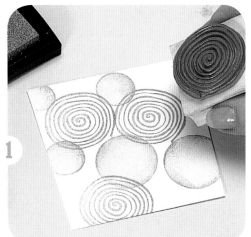

## STEP INSTRUCTION

**ONE** | Trim the white cardstock square into an irregular square, trimming along the edges so the corners aren't right angles. Using gold metallic ink, stamp swirls, spirals and circles randomly over the white cardstock. Leave white space in some areas and overlap images in others.

**TWO** | Color the unstamped areas on the white cardstock using the colored chalks. Blend the colors together, leaving the stamped circles, swirls and spirals uncolored.

**THREE** | Randomly wrap, both horizontally and vertically, the white cardstock with metallic gold thread. Secure the thread with adhesive tape on the back of the cardstock.

**FOUR** | Stamp the Happy New Year message on a scrap of white cardstock using black ink. Highlight the stamped message with lime green ink and a circle stamp, then punch out the message with a ¾" (2cm) circle punch. Punch stars out of purple, gold and metallic gold papers. Glue the white cardstock wrapped in thread to the card. Glue the message to one side, fitting it inside a circle stamp if possible. Finally, mount the stars randomly across the card with mounting tape.

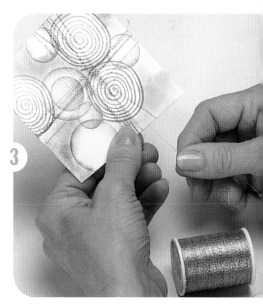

## Tip

Don't throw away beautiful papers, no matter where you find them. Look inside gift certificates, candy boxes and store-bought gifts for metallic tissue paper and other treasures.

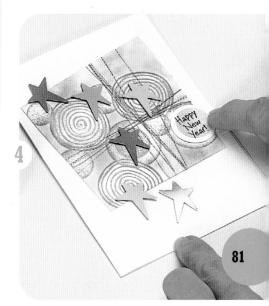

**Materials** ◄ 8½" × 5½" (22cm × 14cm) White cardstock folded to a 4¼" × 5½" (11cm × 14cm) card ‣ Zigzag stitch stamp (HERO ARTS) ‣ X and O letter stamps (HERO ARTS) ‣ Black and red ink ‣ 1" (3cm) Painted wooden heart ‣ Gold heart brad ‣ Glue dots ‣ Wire cutters

seasonal delights cards seasonal delights cards seasonal delights cards seasonal delights card

## Hugs & Kisses

VALENTINE'S DAY SHOULD BE filled with fun and romance. This card has a little of both. No matter how you play the game, whoever receives the card is guaranteed to be the winner!

*This zigzag stamp will keep you in stitches! Stamp it horizontally across the card. Cut slits above and below the stamp to tuck the hearts on the front of the card. Hearts can be stamped in various reds, pinks or white, and can be trimmed before tucking them on the card. Mount one heart with foam tape on top of the others.*

INSPIRATION CORNER

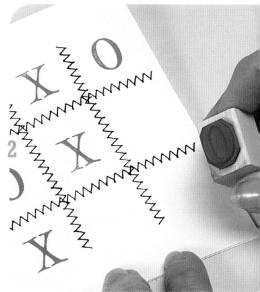

## STEP INSTRUCTION

**ONE** | Create a tic-tac-toe game board by stamping the zigzag stitch stamp on the front of the white card in black ink. Stamp two lines horizontally and two vertically. Make sure there is enough space between the lines for the *X* and *O* letter stamps.

**TWO** | Stamp *X*'s and *O*'s in the squares on the card using the red ink, making sure to leave one square blank.

**THREE** | Cut the back off the gold heart brad using the wire cutters. Make sure the back of the gold heart is flat.

**FOUR** | Using the glue dots, glue the wooden heart in the empty square on the card, and then glue the gold heart inside the wooden heart.

 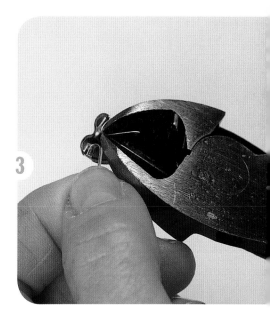

*Try this!*

Make lines for the tic-tac-toe game board with a sewing machine and dark thread.

83

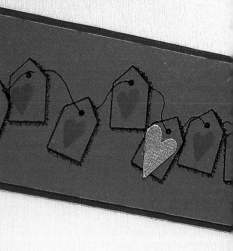

**Materials** ◄ 8½" × 6" (22cm × 15cm) Ivory crepe cardstock folded to a 4¼" × 6" (11cm × 15cm) card ▸ 3½" × 1¾" (9cm × 4cm) Bright red cardstock ▸ Dark red cardstock ▸ Gold metallic paper ▸ Little tag stamp (STAMPENDOUS) ▸ Solid heart stamp (MOSTLY HEARTS) ▸ Black and red ink ▸ Fine-point black marker ▸ Glue stick ▸ Scissors ▸ Small heart punch

asonal delights cards seasonal delights cards seasonal delights cards seasonal delights card
delights cards seasonal delights cards seasonal delights cards seasonal delights cards seaso
seasonal delights cards seasonal delights cards seasonal delights cards seasonal delights c
light cards seasonal delights cards seasonal delights cards seasonal delights cards seasona
asonal delights cards seasonal delights cards seasonal delights cards seasonal delights card

# Heart Tags

SWEET, SIMPLE AND ROMANTIC, let this string of heart tags touch someone's heart this Valentine's Day. It's an easy way to show someone how much you really care.

**INSPIRATION CORNER**

Stampers love tag cards. Ink a large checker board shadow stamp in red and stamp it on a white tag. Stamp solid red hearts, black outline hearts and black tags randomly over the checker board. Stamp tiny red hearts inside the tags. Punch out white paper hearts and glue them to the side of the card. Tie a red ribbon on the top of the tag and glue it on the card.

## STEP INSTRUCTION

**ONE** | Use black ink to stamp a line of little tags across the bright red cardstock. Stamp the tags in a line, but randomly angle and position each tag. Stamp a red heart inside each tag. Leave one tag in the middle of the line without a heart.

**TWO** | Using the fine-point black marker, draw a line through the stamped holes in the top of the tags, so it appears the tags are hanging from the line. The line will enter from the front of the hole and leave from behind the tag.

**THREE** | Punch a heart out of gold metallic paper. Using a glue stick, glue it on the empty tag.

**FOUR** | Assemble the card. Mount the bright red cardstock onto dark red cardstock, and then trim the dark red cardstock to create a 1/8" (3mm) border around the bright red cardstock. Glue the dark red cardstock to the center of the card.

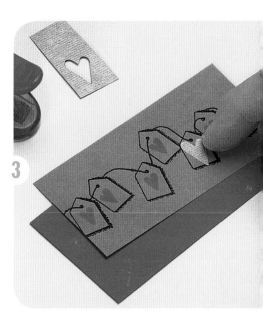

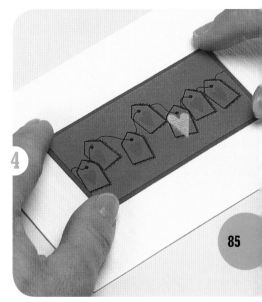

### Tip

When stamping ink on a similarly colored paper, make sure the ink is dark enough to show up against the paper. Sometimes inks get much lighter when they dry.

**Materials◄** 8½" × 5½" (22cm × 14cm) Double-sided pink cardstock folded to a 4¼" × 5½" (11cm × 14cm) card ▸ 3" × 3¾" (8cm × 10cm) Pink striped cardstock ▸ 2" × 2¾" (5cm × 7cm) Red cardstock ▸ Pink cardstock ▸ Tiny heart stamp (MOSTLY HEARTS) ▸ Diamond pattern stamp (HERO ARTS) ▸ Dark pink ink ▸ 10" (25cm) Light pink and dark pink decorative cords ▸ Glue stick ▸ Glue dots ▸ Foam mounting tape ▸ Scallop-edged decorative scissors ▸ Pinking shears ▸ Scissors

asonal delights cards seasonal delights cards seasonal delights cards seasonal delights card delights cards seasonal delights cards seasonal delights cards seasonal delights cards seaso seasonal delights cards seasonal delights cards seasonal delights cards seasonal delights c light cards seasonal de seonal delights cards seasonal delights cards seasona asonal delights cards elights onal delights cards seasonal delights card

# Diamonds & Stripes

SUMPTUOUS REDS, PRETTY PINKS, luxurious diamonds and a touch of decorative cord—what's not to love about this card? Give a card as pretty and striking as this one next Valentine's Day and you're sure to win hugs and kisses.

INSPIRATION CORNER

*Everyone loves hearts! Stamp the diamond pattern stamp in dark red on red paper. Mount the red paper on darker red paper. Punch nine hearts out of various decorative papers or stamped scraps. Glue the hearts onto the diamonds. Glue the red papers on a base card.*

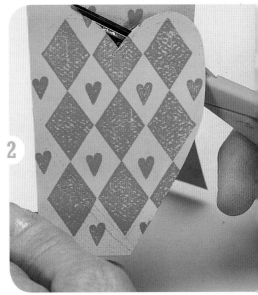

## STEP INSTRUCTION

**ONE** | With the card folded at the top, trim off the bottom ½" (12mm) from the front of the card. Use scallop-edged scissors to trim the bottom of the back of the card. The scallop edge should appear at the bottom when the card is closed.

**TWO** | Using dark pink ink, stamp the diamond pattern on pink cardstock. Using the same dark pink ink, stamp a tiny heart in the open areas between diamonds. When the ink is dry, freehand cut a heart from the stamped cardstock. The diamond pattern should fill the entire heart.

**THREE** | Holding the light pink and dark pink decorative cords together, tie the cords into a single bow.

**FOUR** | Assemble the card. Using a glue stick, glue the striped pink cardstock in the center of the card front. Make sure the stripes are vertical. Next, trim the bottom of the red cardstock using pinking shears and glue it in the middle of the pink striped cardstock. Using mounting tape, mount the heart on the red cardstock. With a glue dot, glue the bow on the heart.

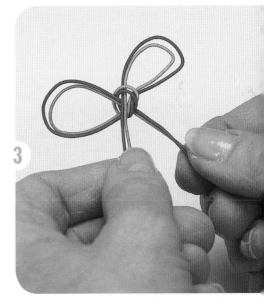

Tip

You may want to lightly sketch a heart on the diamond pattern before cutting it out. When finished, carefully erase the lines.

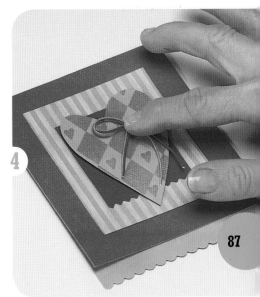

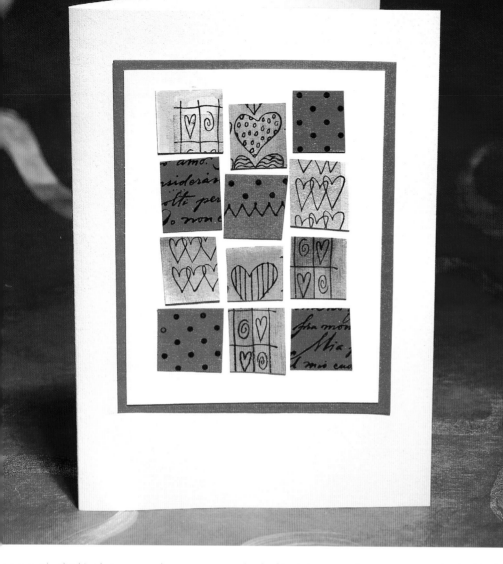

**Materials** ◄ 8½" × 6" (22cm × 15cm) Chalk white cardstock folded to a 4¼" × 6" (11cm × 15cm) card

▸ 3" × 4" (8cm × 10cm) White cardstock

▸ 3¼" × 4¼" (8cm × 11cm) Pink cardstock

▸ White, red and pink cardstock scraps

▸ Various heart and valentine image stamps (HERO ARTS) ▸ Black permanent ink ▸ Red, pink, orange and purple watercolor pencils ▸ Waterbrush pen

▸ Glue stick ▸ Removable tape ▸ Scissors

# Valentine Mosaic

THIS HEARTFELT VALENTINE MOSAIC is an original work of art, lovingly assembled and handmade, to be cherished for many years to come. Try using some of those beautiful papers you've been saving for this card.

INSPIRATION CORNER

88

*Rainbow colored hearts are perfect for any occasion. Stamp a vertical row of hearts in black on the edge of a tall white card. Color the hearts with a watercolor pencil and blend with a waterbrush. When dry, cut around the hearts with sharp scissors to create a scalloped edge.*

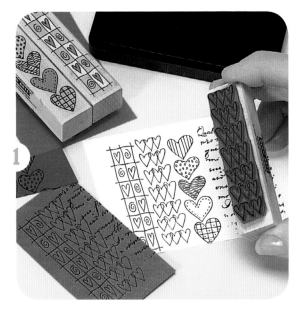

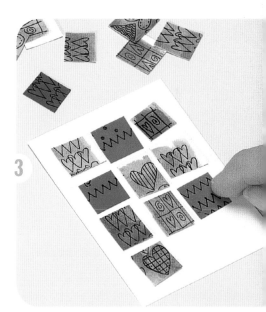

## STEP INSTRUCTION

**ONE** | Randomly stamp the hearts and valentine images with permanent black ink on various scrap white, red and pink cardstock.

**TWO** | Color over all of the heart and valentine images using watercolor pencils, then blend the colors using the waterbrush pen. Be sloppy, there's no reason to stay inside the lines. Let the images dry.

**THREE** | Cut the images into irregular ½" (13mm) squares. Arrange the squares on the white cardstock, balancing colors and images in a pleasing way. Create a rough rectangle with the squares, three squares across and four down. When you are happy with the arrangement, use a glue stick to glue the squares in place. Note: You may want to hold the arrangement together with removeable tape until all the pieces are secured with glue.

**FOUR** | Glue the white cardstock on pink cardstock. Trim the pink cardstock to create a ⅛" (3mm) border around the white cardstock. Glue the pink cardstock to the front of the card.

By stamping on cardstock pieces other than white, the other colors seem more vivid and you have a better contrast between the light and dark colors.

**Materials** ◀ 7" × 4" (18cm × 10cm) Light green cardstock folded to a 3½" × 4" (9cm × 10cm) card ▸ White cardstock ▸ Dark green cardstock ▸ Stripe print stamp (HERO ARTS) ▸ Large and small shamrock stamps (MOSTLY HEARTS) ▸ Green rainbow ink pad ▸ Darker green ink ▸ Glue stick ▸ Mini pinking scissors ▸ Scissors

# Field of Shamrocks

WHAT LUCKY RECIPIENT WILL receive this St. Patrick's day greeting from you? With a field of green and a flurry of shamrocks, this card has more than a touch of the Irish.

*Make this lucky charm card faster than a leprechaun can dance a jig! Use the stripe stamp and green ink to make plaid on white paper. Trim around the plaid, then wrap green ribbon around the rectangle and attach a shamrock charm with a brad. Glue the plaid paper to white, then to green and finally to a larger base card.*

## STEP INSTRUCTION

**ONE** | Create green plaid on the white cardstock. First stamp the stripes in one direction using the green rainbow ink pad. Re-ink, then stamp the same area with the stripes turned 90 degrees.

**TWO** | Cut out the plaid stamped area, trimming the sides to make a rectangle. The rectangle should be about 2" × 2½" (5cm × 6cm). Stamp shamrocks on the plaid using a darker shade of green ink and the large and small shamrock stamps

**THREE** | Glue the plaid stamped cardstock on another piece of white cardstock. Trim the edges of the white cardstock using the mini pinking shears, creating a ⅛" (3mm) border.

**FOUR** | Assemble the card by gluing the white cardstock on top of the dark green cardstock using a glue stick. Trim the edges of the dark green cardstock to create a ⅛" (3mm) border around the white cardstock. Glue the dark green cardstock to the center front of the card.

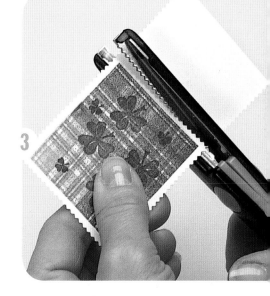

 *Try this!*

If you have one, use a plaid stamp rather than creating your own field of plaid, or use plaid decorative paper.

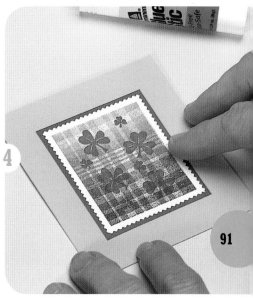

### Materials ◄ 8½" × 5½" (22cm × 14cm) Yellow gold textured cardstock folded to a 4¼" × 5½" (11cm × 14cm) card ▸ 2¼" × 3¼" (6cm × 8cm) White cardstock ▸ 3¾" × 5¼" (10cm × 13cm) White cardstock ▸ Purple cardstock ▸ Easter basket stamp (HERO ARTS) ▸ Easter egg stamps (HERO ARTS) ▸ Black permanent ink ▸ Variety of colored inks ▸ Watercolor pencils ▸ Paintbrush ▸ Palette ▸ Water ▸ Glue stick ▸ Scissors

# Eggs in a Basket

DON'T PUT ALL YOUR EGGS in one basket! Leave some for this fabulous card. Celebrate the coming of spring and Easter with this brightly colored Easter basket card.

### INSPIRATION CORNER

92

*These brightly colored eggs may not be filled with chocolate, but they'll make someone happy when they arrive in the mail. Stamp rows of shadow squares over the card in a light ink color. Stamp egg stamps in the squares using brighter colors. Add an egg charm and ribbon to finish.*

## STEP INSTRUCTION

**ONE** | Stamp the Easter basket in black permanent ink in the center of the smaller white cardstock. Let the ink dry.

**TWO** | Use watercolors to color the Easter basket, bow and eggs (see page 15 for more information on using watercolors).

**THREE** | Stamp a background of Easter eggs on the larger piece of white cardstock. Use a variety of colored inks and egg stamps. Fill the outer edge of the cardstock with eggs, allowing some to extend over the edges and the eggs to overlap. There's no need to stamp the middle of the card.

**FOUR** | Glue the smaller white cardstock with the stamped basket on the purple cardstock using a glue stick. Trim the purple cardstock to create a 1/8" (3mm) border around the white cardstock. Glue the purple cardstock piece to the center of the larger stamped white cardstock piece so the stamped eggs frame it. Finally, glue the larger white cardstock piece to the center front of the yellow gold linen weave card.

*Try this!*

No time to stamp all those tiny background eggs? Stamp the egg basket and enlarge it on a copier to fit the entire card. Stamp a few colorful eggs, cut them out and glue them in the basket.

93

Materials ◄ 6" × 6" (15cm × 15cm) Chalk white cardstock folded to a 3" × 6" (8cm × 15cm) card ▸ 3" × ½" (8cm × 13mm) Pink cardstock ▸ White cardstock scrap ▸ Circle stamp (HERO ARTS) ▸ Bunny stamp (HERO ARTS) ▸ Black and lime green ink ▸ Light pink marker ▸ 3" (8cm) Pink and white gingham ribbon ▸ Glue stick ▸ Glue dots ▸ Foam mounting tape ▸ Scissors ▸ Scallop-edged scissors

# Here Comes the Bunny!

LET THIS PLAYFUL LITTLE bunny help usher in spring! Around him you'll find soft pinks and greens, scallop edging and pink gingham ribbon.

INSPIRATION CORNER

94

*Purple and yellow are traditionally Easter colors. Look through your unused paint chips for colors that will work for the season. Stamp the bunny on a two-toned lavender chip and glue it on purple and gold paper. Glue this on a larger yellow card and add a matching bow.*

## STEP INSTRUCTION

**ONE** | Trim the bottom ¼" (6mm) from the front of the card using the scallop-edged decorative scissors. Using a glue stick, glue the pink cardstock inside the card over the trimmed edge, so the pink appears at the bottom front of the card. Trim the pink even with the back of the card.

**TWO** | Stamp a lime green circle centered in the upper half of the card front.

**THREE** | Stamp the bunny on a scrap of white cardstock using black ink. Cut out the bunny, then color in the ear with a light pink marker.

**FOUR** | Attach the bunny in the middle of the green circle on the card using mounting tape. Tie a knot in the ribbon and trim the edges to the desired length. Attach the ribbon below the bunny using a glue dot.

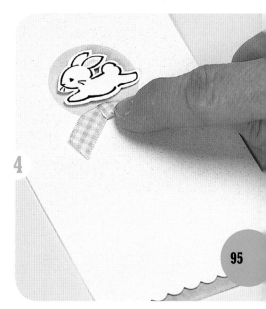

*Try this!*

Why not turn the card so it opens horizontally? You'll have room to stamp an entire row of bunnies.

**Materials** ◄ 8½" × 5½" (22cm × 14cm) White cardstock folded to a 4¼" × 5½" (11cm × 14cm) card ▸ 2⅜" × 3¾" (6cm × 10cm) White cardstock ▸ Pink cardstock ▸ Deckle-edged square stamp (HERO ARTS) ▸ Bouquet of flowers stamp (HERO ARTS) ▸ Aqua, pink, lime, orange-yellow and lavender inks ▸ Black permanent ink ▸ Watercolor markers ▸ 3" (8cm) Stitched satin ribbon ▸ Glue stick ▸ Glue dots ▸ Paintbrush ▸ Palette ▸ Water ▸ Scissors

# Bouquet for Mother

MOM DESERVES MORE than a store-bought card. Celebrate Mother's Day with the bouquet of flowers on this handmade card. Give it to her whether she is near or far (though if she's near, I'd suggest accompanying it with a hug).

## INSPIRATION CORNER

*Try using the flower stamp in a completely different way. Stamp the flowers only in black ink around the edges of a white square. Softly color the flowers with watercolors. Stamp a message on a scrap of paper, glue it in the middle of the card and add an embellishment. Frame it on coordinating paper and then glue it on printed cardstock.*

## STEP INSTRUCTION

**ONE** | Use the deckle-edged square stamp to randomly stamp deckled squares to cover the front of the card. Use a variety of inks, letting the edges of the squares slightly overlap.

**TWO** | Stamp the bouquet of flowers using black permanent ink in the center of the white cardstock. Let the ink dry.

**THREE** | Color the bouquet of flowers using watercolors. Blend the colors using a paintbrush and water (see page 15 for more information on using watercolors).

**FOUR** | Assemble the card. Using the glue stick, glue the white cardstock on a piece of pink cardstock. Trim the pink cardstock to create a ⅛" (3mm) border around the white. Glue the pink cardstock to the center of the stamped card. Tie a knot in the stitched ribbon and use a glue dot to attach it to the top of the vase.

*Try this!*

For even more pizzazz, add tiny buttons, rhinestones, glitter or other embellishments to the centers of the flowers.

**Materials** ◄ 8½" × 6" (22cm × 15cm) Burgundy cardstock folded to a 4¼" × 6" (11cm x 15cm) card ► 1¾" × 2⅛" (4cm × 5cm) Beige cardstock ► 2¾" × 3½" (7cm × 9cm) Beige cardstock ► 3" × 4¼" (8cm × 11cm) Red striped paper ► Ivory cardstock ► Metallic gold paper ► Stripes stamp (HERO ARTS) ► Father's Day stamp (MOSTLY HEARTS) ► Black ink ► Red and brown watercolor markers ► Raffia ► 6" (15cm) Jute ► Bronze button ► Four gold photo corners ► Glue stick ► Glue dots ► Scissors ► Sewing machine and thread (optional)

# A Tribute to Dad

DADS DESERVE THEIR SPECIAL day too! Give him a card that he'll be proud to display. Fishing lures, power tools and comfortable slippers are optional, but a tribute to dear old dad isn't.

INSPIRATION CORNER

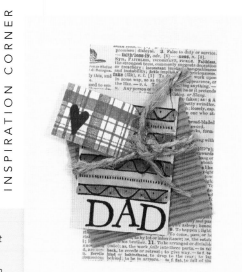

*Here's another special card for dad. Gather paper scraps and collage them on a neutral-colored card. Use an alphabet stamp to add text, the stripes stamp to make plaid and a punched out heart for a final touch. Wrap up the collage with jute before attaching it to the card.*

*Try this!*

Why not use a new fishing lure instead of the jute and button on the front of the card?

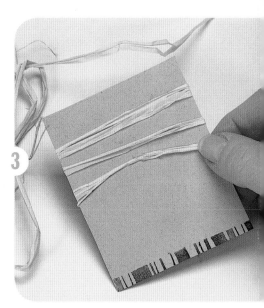

## STEP INSTRUCTION

**ONE** | Ink with a brown marker and stamp the stripes on the smaller piece of beige cardstock. Clean the stamp, then use the red marker to re-ink the stamp. Turn the stamp 90 degrees and stamp the beige cardstock again. This should create a plaid pattern.

**TWO** | Apply gold photo corner stickers to the corners of the smaller beige cardstock that's been stamped with a plaid pattern.

**THREE** | Use the brown marker and the stripe stamp to stamp the bottom ¼" (6mm) of the larger beige cardstock. Wrap three strings of raffia around the top of the cardstock. Wrap the first piece ½" (12mm) from the top and leaving ¼" (6mm) between each piece. Use a glue dot on the back of the cardstock to hold the raffia in place. Trim the excess raffia. If desired, stitch the raffia in place with a sewing machine.

**FOUR** | Glue gold metallic paper to one edge of the printed cardstock, creating a ⅛" (3mm) border. Trim the edges of the gold paper even with the printed cardstock. Stamp a Happy Father's Day message using black ink on ivory cardstock, then trim the cardstock around the message.

**FIVE** | Assemble the card. Lay the printed cardstock at an angle on the card front, then lay the beige cardstock with raffia at an angle on top of it. Angle the plaid cardstock over the raffia. Place the stamped Father's Day note at the bottom. When satisfied with the placement, glue the pieces in place with a glue stick. Finally, use a glue dot to attach a bronze button with jute folded behind it on the plaid cardstock.

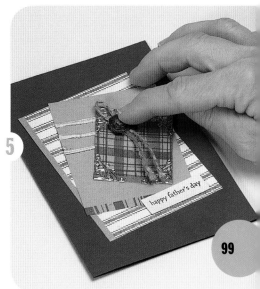

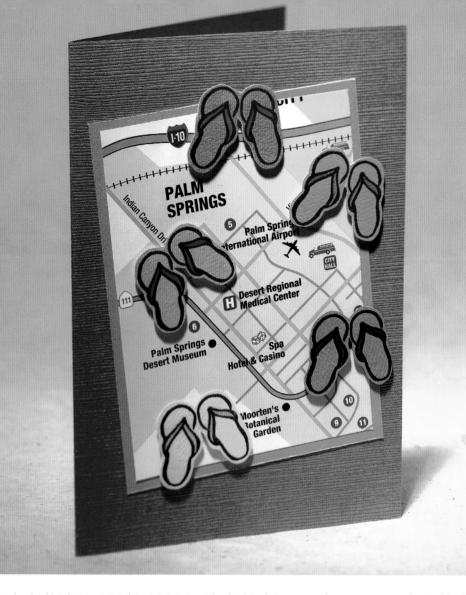

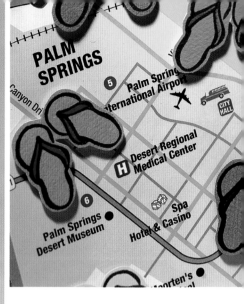

**Materials** ◀ 8½" × 6" (22cm × 15cm) Turquoise Tsumugi cardstock folded to a 4¼" × 6" (11cm x 15cm) card ▸ 3¼" × 4¼" (8cm × 11cm) Section of a map (of a vacation location) ▸ Light green cardstock (or another color of your choosing) ▸ Various colorful paper scraps ▸ Beach border stamp (STAMPENDOUS) ▸ Black ink ▸ Colored markers ▸ Glue stick ▸ Foam mounting tape ▸ Scissors

seasonal delights cards seasonal delights cards seasonal delights cards seasonal delights cards seasonal delights cards seasonal delights cards seasonal delights cards seasonal delights cards seasonal delights cards seasonal delights cards seasonal delights cards seasonal delights cards seasonal delights cards seasonal delights cards seasonal delights cards seasonal delights cards seasonal delights cards seasonal delights cards seasonal delights card

# On the Go

HELP A FRIEND START summer vacation on the right foot with this card! One look at the path of these sandals and a smile is guaranteed to follow.

## INSPIRATION CORNER

*Here's a shout out to summer fun! Stamp the summer border stamp in black on a strip of white paper. Ink a large circle stamp and stamp over the summer images using different colored inks. Glue this on coordinating paper and glue it to a base card. Glue a punched out circle of yellow paper in the sun.*

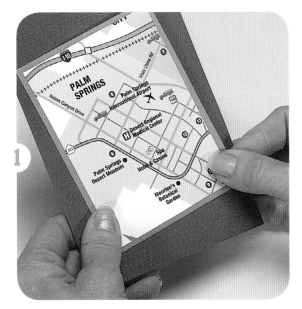

## STEP INSTRUCTION

**ONE** | Cut out a 3¼" x 4¼" (8cm x 11cm) section of a map and glue it on light green (or coordinating color) cardstock using a glue stick. Trim the cardstock to create a ⅛" (3mm) border around the map. Position the cardstock and map on the center front of the card, turning it slightly to find a pleasing position, then glue it in place.

**TWO** | Stamp the sandals on scraps of colorful paper using black ink. Color the straps with colored markers. Cut out the sandals from the paper.

**THREE** | Mount the sandals randomly across the map using foam mounting tape. Add rhinestones, beads or tiny flowers to the sandals if desired.

Try this!

Pick up free maps at visitor centers while on vacation, then personalize the card by choosing a map that means something special to the card recipient. Or use a mapping program to find a map and print it out in color.

**101**

Materials◄ 7" × 5½" (18cm × 14cm) White cardstock folded to a 3½" × 5½ (9cm × 14cm) card ▸ Printed blue, green and yellow paper with polka dots ▸ Blue, green and yellow cardstock (the colors should be darker than the printed paper) ▸ White cardstock scrap ▸ Gingham ribbon stamp (HERO ARTS) ▸ Beach stamps (MOSTLY HEARTS) ▸ Frame stamp (MOSTLY HEARTS) ▸ Black ink ▸ Glue stick ▸ Foam mounting tape ▸ Scissors ▸ Mini pinking scissors

asonal delights cards seasonal delights cards seasonal delights cards seasonal delights card
delights cards seasonal delights cards seasonal delights cards seasonal delights cards seaso
seasonal delights cards seasonal delights cards seasonal delights cards seasonal delights c
light cards seasonal delights cards seasonal delights cards seasonal delights cards seasona
asonal delights cards seasonal delights cards seasonal delights cards seasonal delights card

# Surf's Up

WATCH OUT FOR THE WAVES! This card is perfect for a quick summer vacation note. The brightly colored beach images tumbling down the card create the illusion of a wave, guaranteed to make a friend jealous while you enjoy the sand and sun.

## INSPIRATION CORNER

*Calling all beach bums! Stamp out a handful of these cards for a hostess gift before you arrive at a friend's beach house. Stamp a light blue square and then stamp beach images in black. Stamp the beach ball on a scrap of light blue, then attach it with a brad. Trim and glue the square on coordinating paper, then glue this on a printed card with a gingham ribbon loop tucked at the top.*

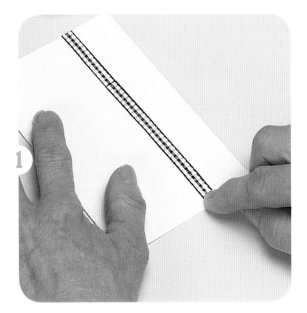

## STEP INSTRUCTION

**ONE** | Stamp the gingham ribbon with black ink on a scrap of white paper. Cut out the ribbon and glue it on the front of the card, 1" (3cm) from the right edge. Trim the top and bottom of the strip flush with the edges of the card.

**TWO** | Create the "postage stamps." Use black ink to stamp the frame on each color of printed paper. Stamp the beach images in the middle of the frame using black ink. Create three such "postage stamps" using the beach images.

**THREE** | Cut a square around each of the stamped images using the mini pinking scissors. Glue the stamped squares on the darker colored cardstock with a glue stick. Trim to create a $\frac{1}{8}$" (3mm) border around the stamped square.

**FOUR** | Arrange the postage stamps in a haphazard fashion down the gingham border, then use mounting tape to secure them in place.

*Try this!*

Stamp and decorate your envelope to match the card and find a color coordinated postage stamp. You'll be amazed at the reactions you'll get from recipients who receive a decorated envelope in the mail.

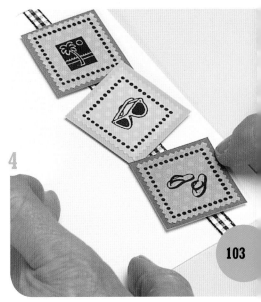

103

M a t e r i a l s ◂ 10½" × 5¼" (27cm × 13cm) White cardstock folded to a 5¼" (13cm) square card ▸ 3" × 3½" (8cm × 9cm) Orange cardstock ▸ Bright green, gold, red and purple scraps of paper ▸ Palm tree, golf tee, sun and beach chair stamps (MOSTLY HEARTS) ▸ Black ink ▸ Square orange button ▸ Glue stick ▸ Glue dots ▸ Sewing machine or needle and orange thread ▸ Pinking shears ▸ Scissors

seasonal delights cards seasonal delights cards seasonal delights cards seasonal delights cards
delights cards seasonal delights cards seasonal delights cards seasonal delights cards seaso
seasonal delights cards seasonal delights cards seasonal delights cards seasonal delights card
light cards seasonal delights cards seasonal delights cards seasonal delights cards seasona
sonal delights cards seasonal delights cards seasonal delights cards seasonal delights card

# Happy Days Ahead!

WE ALL LOVE THE LAZY days of summer. Why not celebrate doing absolutely nothing, carefree moments and bright sunny days on the beach with this card?

INSPIRATION CORNER

This card makes an excellent retirement card or a cover for a travel journal. Ink an irregular shadow stamp with warm colors and stamp it on ivory. Stamp the travel images in black. Trim, leaving a tiny border of ivory. Glue this to a collage of printed travel papers, copper ridged paper and grasscloth paper scraps. Add eyelets to one of the papers, then assemble them on a burgundy card. Tie jute in a bow and adhere it with a glue dot.

## STEP INSTRUCTION

**ONE** | Stamp the palm tree, golf tee, sun and beach chair stamps using black ink on bright green, gold, red and purple scraps of paper.

**TWO** | Cut out the images in haphazard squares. Position the squares together in a larger, irregular square. Trim the edges of the smaller squares that make up the larger square so the stamped images fit together neatly and without overlapping.

**THREE** | Trim the edges of the orange cardstock with pinking shears. Use a sewing machine or a needle to perforate the cardstock to create a border of regularly spaced holes ¼" (6mm) from the edge. Make sure to work over a soft surface if not using a sewing machine.

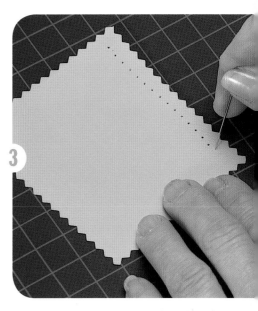

**FOUR** | Sew the four stamped squares, pieced together into a larger, irregular square, onto the orange cardstock using a needle or sewing machine and orange thread. Make stitches where the individual squares connect. Do not stitch the outside edges of the squares.

**FIVE** | Assemble the card by using a glue stick to glue the orange cardstock to the front of the card, then use a glue dot to attach an orange square button to the upper right corner of the orange cardstock.

A mouse pad makes an excellent soft surface for perforating the cardstock with a needle tool or a large darning needle.

105

Materials◀ 8½" × 5½" (22cm × 14cm) Speckled beige cardstock folded to a 4¼" × 5½" (11cm × 14cm) card ▸ ¼" × 5½"(6mm × 14cm) Black strip of paper ▸ Red, orange and yellow paper ▸ Leaves and jack-o'-lanterns stamps (STAMPENDOUS) ▸ Black ink ▸ Glue stick ▸ Foam mounting tape ▸ Scissors

sonal delights cards seasonal delights cards seasonal delights cards seasonal delights card
delights cards seasonal delights cards seasonal delights cards seasonal delights cards seaso
seasonal delights cards seasonal delights cards seasonal delights cards seasonal delights c
ights cards seasonal delights cards seasonal delights cards seasonal delights cards seasona
sonal delights card seasonal delights cards seasonal delights cards seasonal delights cards

# Autumn Greeting

USE YOUR AUTUMN-COLORED paper scraps to make this quick and easy card. Why not send it as a celebration of the season, or as a friendly greeting? The colors and fun seasonal images will brighten anyone's day!

INSPIRATION CORNER

*Jolly jack-o'-lanterns will light up a dark fall evening! Stamp these cheery faces in black onto a pale orange checkerboard background. Scatter leaves among the pumpkins. Stamp yellow and orange geometric squares. Knot a trick or treat ribbon and glue it to the card.*

## STEP INSTRUCTION

**ONE** | Using black ink, stamp leaf and jack-o'-lantern images on red, orange and yellow paper.

**TWO** | Cut the paper in squares around the images. Try to keep the squares about the same size if possible. Glue the images on pieces of coordinating colored paper using a glue stick. Trim the coordinating colored paper around the square to create a ⅛" (3mm) border.

**THREE** | Glue the black strip vertically on the card front, 1¼" (3cm) from the right edge of the card. Trim the top and bottom of the strip even with the edges of the card.

**FOUR** | Place the stamped blocks of paper along the black strip. Lay them slightly overlapping, randomly tilting the blocks for a decorative effect. When you are pleased with the arrangement, use foam mounting tape to secure them. If necessary, make more of the stamped blocks to create the arrangement you like.

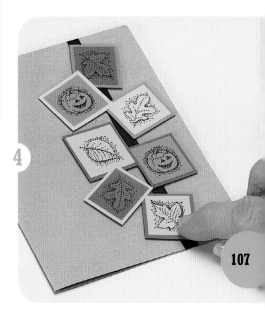

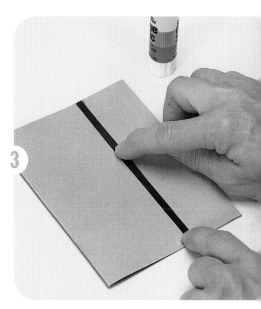

*Try this!*

Add depth to the images by coloring them with colored pencils or watercolors.

107

## Materials ◄ 8½" × 5½" (22cm × 14cm) Brown woven texture cardstock folded to a 4¼" × 5½" (11cm × 14cm) card ▸ 3½" × 4¾" (9cm × 12cm) Metallic copper paper ▸ 3¼" × 4½" (8cm × 11cm) Tan speckled paper ▸ 2½" × 3¾" (6cm × 10cm) Ivory cardstock ▸ Golden wheat stamp (HERO ARTS) ▸ Leaf stamp (HERO ARTS) ▸ Watermark ink ▸ Gold embossing powder ▸ 5½" (14cm) Brown double-sided satin ribbon ▸ Glue stick ▸ Glue dots ▸ Scissors ▸ Heat gun

# Golden Wheat

EMBOSSING IS A SIMPLE WAY to add a glamorous touch to your cards. Rich browns and golds, a touch of ribbon and a watermark ink background make this a luxurious card that you can create in no time, but that is sure to impress.

INSPIRATION CORNER

*The brilliance in autumn colors is astounding! Gather leaf stamps and stamp them across white paper using watermark ink. Use chalks to blend fall colors across the white paper. Glue the white paper on gold, and then on a handmade leaf paper card.*

## STEP INSTRUCTION

**ONE** | Stamp the golden wheat in the center of the ivory cardstock using watermark ink. Sprinkle gold embossing powder over the wet ink and remove the excess, then heat the powder with the heat gun (see page 14 for more information on embossing).

**TWO** | Ink the edge of the ivory cardstock with watermark ink, then emboss the edges with gold powder using the heat gun.

**THREE** | Stamp a background with the leaf stamp on the tan paper using watermark ink. Fill the paper with the images, letting some of the images extend over the sides of the paper. This effect will be very subtle.

**FOUR** | Assemble the card. Glue the embossed ivory cardstock in the center of the tan paper using the glue stick. Glue the tan paper in the center of the copper paper. Glue the copper paper in the center front of the brown card. Knot the brown satin ribbon and glue it on the left side of the card with a glue dot under the knot. Trim the ribbon as desired.

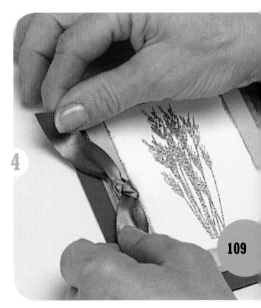

*Tip*

Watermark ink gives you a great tone-on-tone effect on paper, and can also double as embossing ink.

## Materials ◄ 9" × 6" (23cm × 15cm) Handmade straw paper folded to a 4½" × 6" (11cm × 15cm) card
▸ 3" × 4¼" (8cm × 11cm) Script text decorative paper ▸ 2¾" × 4" (7cm × 10cm) Printed text decorative paper
▸ 2" × 3" (5cm × 8cm) Ivory cardstock
▸ Red, orange and rust-colored paper
▸ Solid leaf stamp (POSH IMPRESSIONS)
▸ Outline leaf stamp (POSH IMPRESSIONS)
▸ Black ink ▸ Golden yellow ink ▸ 5" (13cm) Twine ▸ Glue stick ▸ Foam mounting tape ▸ Scissors

asonal delights cards seasonal delights cards seasonal delights cards seasonal delights card
delights cards seasonal delights cards seasonal delights cards seasonal delights cards seasc
seasonal delights cards seasonal delights cards seasonal delights cards seasonal delights c
lights cards seasonal delights cards seasonal delights cards seasonal delights cards seasona
asonal delights cards seasonal delights cards seasonal delights cards seasonal delights card

# Falling Leaves

FALL HAS ALWAYS BEEN a celebration of color. On this card, leaves tumble gracefully in a dance of color. A bit of twine, printed papers and handmade straw paper make the perfect setting for these fall colors.

**INSPIRATION CORNER**

*Let these fall leaves fill your paper with autumn colors! Use the solid leaf stamp with brilliant colored ink, markers or paints to get a gorgeous blend of color. Glue the stamped leaves paper to a complementary colored background and a base card. Add glitter to the leaves to make them glisten.*

## STEP INSTRUCTION

**ONE** | Randomly stamp the solid leaf over the ivory colored cardstock using golden yellow ink. To create a variety of color depths on the ivory cardstock, don't ink the stamp after each use. Overlap the images, and let some run off the edges of the cardstock.

**TWO** | Stamp the outline leaf on the red, orange and rust-colored paper using black ink. Cut out the leaf images, leaving a small border of paper.

**THREE** | Place the smaller printed text paper centered over the larger script text paper, then glue the larger in the center front of the card using a glue stick. Place the stamped ivory cardstock in the middle, angling it over the printed paper. Glue the ivory cardstock in place when you are pleased with the position. Place the twine vertically over the layered papers, positioning it as you like. Use glue to hold the twine in place. Position the cut leaves on the twine.

**FOUR** | When you are satisfied with the position of the leaves, secure them along the twine using mounting tape.

*Tip*

Save time! Stamp several pages of leaf images. Cut and trim them when you're watching TV, then save the leaves in a bag for future projects.

111

### Materials ◄ 8½" × 5½" (22cm × 14cm) Speckled beige cardstock folded to a 4¼" × 5½" (11cm × 14cm) card ▸ 2¾" (7cm) Square speckled ivory cardstock ▸ Speckled beige cardstock ▸ Rust-colored cardstock ▸ Red and orange paper ▸ Leaf stamp (HERO ARTS) ▸ Circle stamp (HERO ARTS) ▸ Gold, orange and red watercolor markers ▸ Fine-tip black marker ▸ 4" (10cm) raffia ▸ Glue stick ▸ Foam mounting tape ▸ Sewing machine or needle and orange thread ▸ Scissors ▸ ½" (13mm) Circle punch

seasonal delights cards seasonal delights cards seasonal delights cards seasonal delights cards
delights cards seasonal delights cards seasonal delights cards seasonal delights cards seaso
seasonal delights cards seasonal delights cards seasonal delights cards seasonal delights
lights cards seasonal delights cards seasonal delights cards seasonal delights cards seasona
asonal delights cards seasonal delights cards seasonal delights cards seasonal delights card

# The Turkey Trot

THIS DANCIN' LITTLE TURKEY will make anyone's Thanksgiving even more festive! Clever use of a leaf stamp helps make him unique. You could also use this turkey for notecards, placecards or on napkins for a special family holiday.

*Use this stylish card for Thanksgiving, fall birthdays, thank-you notes and more! Stamp a distressed background with a blend of warm ink colors. Stamp several leaf images over the background. Trim, leaving a tiny white border. Glue it on a red and orange background, then tie raffia over the papers. Finally, glue this to a corrugated card.*

## STEP INSTRUCTION

**ONE** | Ink the leaf stamp with the watercolor markers, blending the colors on the stamp and making sure not to color the stem. When finished, stamp the leaf in the center of the speckled ivory cardstock.

**TWO** | Color the circle stamp with the gold marker and stamp a circle in the lower center of the leaf. This will be the turkey's body. Create a head for the turkey by punching out a ½" (13mm) circle from speckled beige cardstock. Freehand tear a small gobbler from red paper. Freehand cut a nose from orange paper. Glue them both to the face with a glue stick. Add eyes with the fine-tip black marker. Mount the head above the body with foam mounting tape.

**THREE** | Draw legs on the turkey using the fine-tip marker.

**FOUR** | Glue the ivory cardstock to the rust-colored cardstock using a glue stick. Trim the edges of the rust-colored cardstock to create a ⅛" (3mm) border around the ivory. Angle the rust-colored cardstock on the front of the beige card, then glue it in place. Using orange thread and a zigzag stitch, stitch raffia in a wavy arc above the turkey. Trim the raffia when finished.

Watercolor marker ink dries more slowly than permanent marker ink, allowing better color blending on the stamp. If the ink appears too dry, spritz it with water from a misting bottle before stamping.

**M a t e r i a l s** ◄ 8½" × 5½" (22cm × 14cm) Textured white cardstock folded to a 4¼" × 5½" (11cm × 14cm) card ▸ 2¾" × 4" (7cm × 10cm) White cardstock ▸ White cardstock scrap ▸ Royal blue cardstock ▸ Snowman stamp (HERO ARTS) ▸ Snowy background block stamp (HERO ARTS) ▸ Two shades of blue ink ▸ Black permanent ink ▸ Watercolor pencils ▸ 8" (20cm) Double-edged satin ribbon ▸ Glue stick ▸ Foam mounting tape ▸ Needle tool or sewing machine ▸ Scissors ▸ Paintbrush ▸ Water

asonal delights cards seasonal delights cards seasonal delights cards seasonal delights card
delights cards seasonal delights cards seasonal delights cards seasonal delights cards seaso
seasonal delights cards seasonal delights cards seasonal delights cards seasonal delights c
light cards seasonal delights cards seasonal delights cards seasonal delights cards seasona
asonal delights cards seasonal delights cards seasonal delights cards seasonal delights card

# One Jolly Snowman

WHAT WOULD WINTER BE without a jolly snowman? This guy will never melt, but he's sure to melt hearts when he appears in a mailbox. Build him near a warm fire with a cup of hot chocolate close by.

**INSPIRATION CORNER**

*Snowflake cards can be used all winter, not just at holiday time. Stamp the snowy background stamp side-by-side in blue and purple ink. Trim, leaving a small white border. Punch out snowflakes and place them on the background, then cover the background and snowflakes with a sheer white organdy ribbon, sewing it in place with a zigzag stitch. Trim the ribbon, then glue the snowy background to the textured blue card.*

## STEP INSTRUCTION

**ONE** | Stamp the snowman on a scrap of white cardstock using black ink. Color the hat and scarf using watercolor pencils, then blend the colors using a paintbrush and water (see page 15 for more information on using watercolors). Cut out the snowman when the watercolors are dry.

**TWO** | Stamp the snowy background on the white cardstock rectangle. Stamp the image twice, side by side, in the center of the cardstock using two shades of blue ink. When the ink is dry, make a border of perforated holes around the snowy background using the needle tool or sewing machine, then trim the excess white paper around the holes.

**THREE** | Tie the ribbon around the snowman's neck for a scarf. Trim the ribbon if necessary.

**FOUR** | Mount the snowman to the center of the snowy background using foam mounting tape. Glue the stamped white cardstock to the royal blue cardstock using a glue stick. Trim the royal blue cardstock to create a $\frac{1}{8}$" (3mm) border around the white cardstock. Glue the royal blue cardstock to the center front of the textured white card.

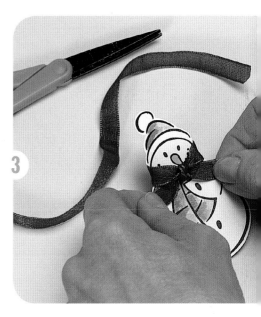

*Try this!*

Add sparkle to the snow and snowman with glitter or glitter glue.

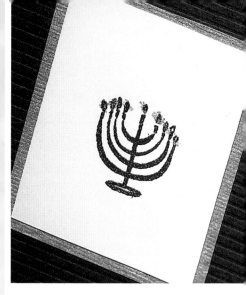

**M a t e r i a l s** ◂ 7" × 7" (18cm × 18cm)
Textured blue paper folded to a 3½" × 7"
(9cm × 18cm) card ▸ 1¾" × 2⅛" (4cm ×
5cm) Ivory cardstock ▸ Metallic gold paper
▸ Menorah candles stamp (HERO ARTS)
▸ Embossing ink ▸ Gold embossing powder
▸ Gold glitter ▸ Glue stick ▸ Gold glitter
glue ▸ Scissors ▸ Heat gun ▸ Tweezers

seasonal delights cards seasonal delights cards seasonal delights cards seasonal delights card
delights cards seasonal delights cards seasonal delights cards seasonal delights cards seaso
seasonal delights cards seasonal delights cards seasonal delights cards seasonal delights ca
ights cards seasonal delights cards seasonal delights cards seasonal delights cards seasona
sonal delights cards seasonal delights cards seasonal delights cards seasonal delights card

# Happy Hanukkah!

LET THIS PRETTY MENORAH light up the eight
days of Hanukkah. This simple card keeps the
focus on the holiday. Embossing adds elegance to
this wonderful holiday of lights.

**INSPIRATION CORNER**

116

*Celebrating the holiday couldn't be easier! Stamp out
the Hanukkah images in black on blue and gold scraps of
paper. Trim the scraps into uneven squares, then arrange
the squares on white cardstock and glue them in place.
Glue this to blue paper, and then to a white ribbed card.*

## STEP INSTRUCTION

**ONE** | Stamp the menorah in the center of the ivory cardstock using embossing ink. Emboss the menorah using the heat gun and gold embossing powder (see page 14 for more information on embossing).

**TWO** | Glue the ivory cardstock on the metallic gold paper using a glue stick. Trim the edges of the gold paper to create a $\frac{1}{8}$" (3mm) border around the ivory cardstock. Glue the gold paper centered near the top of the blue card.

**THREE** | Add glitter glue to the top of the candles on the menorah. For added sparkle, sprinkle more glitter into the glitter glue before it dries.

*Try this!*

Create extra stamped menorahs for placecards and decorations for your holiday celebrations.

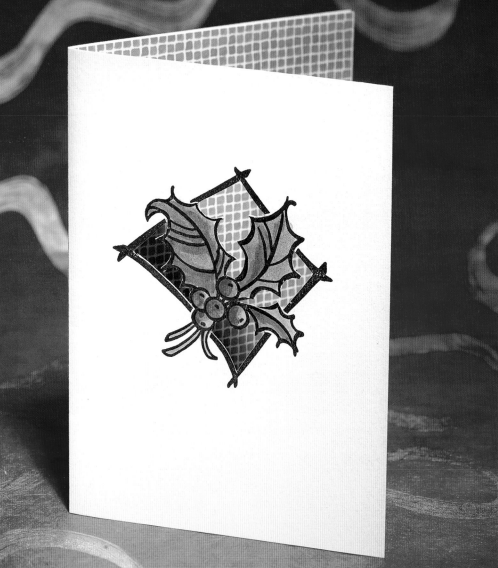

seasonal delights cards seasonal delights cards seasonal delights cards seasonal delights cards delights cards seasonal delights cards seasonal delights cards seasonal delights cards seaso seasonal delights cards seasonal delights cards seasonal delights cards seasonal delights ca ights cards seasonal delights cards seasonal delights cards seasonal delights cards seasonal sonal delights cards seasonal delights cards seasonal delights cards seasonal delights cards

## Materials

<8½" × 6" (22cm × 15cm) Chalk white cardstock folded to a 4¼" × 6" (11cm × 15cm) card • 4¼" × 6" (11cm × 15cm) Green decorative paper • Holly stamp (STAMPENDOUS) • Black permanent ink • Red and green watercolor markers • Glue stick • Paintbrush • Palette • Water • Craft knife and cutting surface>

# Holly-day Cheer

SHINY GREEN HOLLY LEAVES and bright red berries deliver plenty of holiday cheer. This clever greeting allows the printed paper inside the card to to peek from behind the holly to create a fascinating and festive background.

INSPIRATION CORNER

*Greens, golds and reds are rich, traditional holiday colors. Emboss the holly in gold on a green tag. Color the holly with markers and tie a mesh gold bow on top. Glue the tag at an angle on an ivory card.*

118

## STEP INSTRUCTION

**ONE** | Using black permanent ink, stamp the holly on the front of the card, just slightly above the center. Stamp so the holly sits diagonally on the card front. Let the ink dry.

**TWO** | Using red and green watercolor markers, a palette, paintbrush and water, color in the green leaves and red berries of the holly (see page 15 for more information on using watercolors).

**THREE** | Open the card. Place the card on a protected cutting surface, then use a craft knife to cut out the areas around the holly and inside the stamped area.

**FOUR** | On the right side of the opened card, glue the green decorative paper using a glue stick. Trim the decorative paper even with the edges of the card. Make sure the green decorative paper shows through the open windows of the holly.

 Tip

For added depth in your watercoloring projects, paint a first layer and let it dry completely. Paint a second layer in areas you want to highlight. The second layer will be darker than the original layer.

**Materials** ◂ 8½" × 5½" (22cm × 14cm) Double-sided printed green paper folded to a 4¼" × 5½" (11cm × 14cm) card ▸ 3¼" × 4¼" (8cm × 11cm) Speckled oatmeal cardstock ▸ Red and green card-stock ▸ Pine bough stamp (HERO ARTS) ▸ Green ink ▸ Brown watercolor marker ▸ 10" (25cm) Green and red gingham ribbon ▸ Glue stick ▸ Glue dots ▸ Scissors

sonal delights cards seasonal delights cards seasonal delights cards seasonal delights cards
delights cards seasonal delights cards seasonal delights cards seasonal delights cards seaso
seasonal delights cards seasonal delights cards seasonal delights cards seasonal delights ca
ight cards seasonal delights cards seasonal delights cards seasonal delights cards seasonal
sonal delights seasonal ghts cards seasonal delights cards seasonal delights cards

# Holiday Pine

THE SUDDEN APPEARANCE OF a Christmas tree in the living room is a sure sign of the upcoming holiday. This pine branch makes a beautiful card, even without ornaments. Close your eyes and imagine the presents waiting beneath the boughs of your Christmas tree!

INSPIRATION CORNER

*People love to date their holiday cards, especially if they save them from year to year. This tag was stamped with green and brown markers and the year was stamped in black. Tie a satin bow around the tag and add jute through the top hole. Glue the tag on a sage card.*

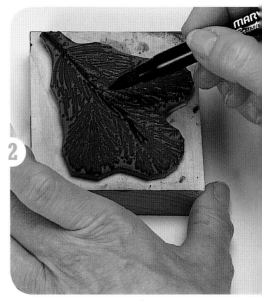

## STEP INSTRUCTION

**ONE** | Cut the bottom ½" (13mm) from the front of the double-sided green card. This will reveal the second pattern inside the card.

**TWO** | Prepare the pine bough stamp by covering the needles in green ink, then coloring in the stem with a brown watercolor marker. Work quickly so the ink doesn't dry.

**THREE** | Stamp the pine bough in the center of the speckled oatmeal cardstock.

**FOUR** | Glue the stamped oatmeal cardstock on the green cardstock using a glue stick. Trim the green to create a ⅛" (3mm) border around the oatmeal. Glue the green on the red cardstock and trim the red to create a ⅛" (3mm) border around the green cardstock. Glue the red cardstock to the center of the green card. Tie a bow in the ribbon, trimming it to the desired length, then use a glue dot to attach the bow to the top of the stamped pine bough.

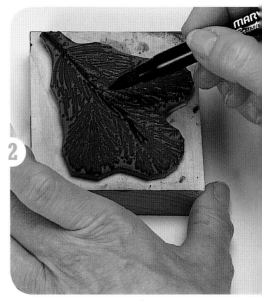

Why not add to the fun and adorn the pine with rhinestones, glitter glue or a tiny charm?

121

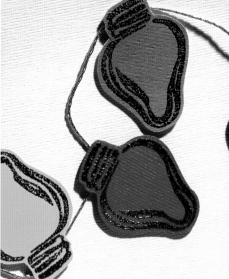

**Materials** ◄ 7" × 5" (18cm × 13cm) Deckle-edged ivory card (can be purchased precut and prefolded, or see page 71 for information on making your own deckle-edged card) ▸ Red, green, blue, purple and yellow cardstock scraps ▸ Holiday light stamp (POSH IMPRESSIONS) ▸ Gold ink ▸ Red watercolor marker ▸ Gold embossing powder ▸ Gold leafing pen ▸ 12" (30cm) Gold cord ▸ Foam mounting tape ▸ Heat gun ▸ Scissors

# Season of Lights

TWINKLING CHRISTMAS LIGHTS ARE a favorite holiday sight. Let these lights brighten up your card and add color to your holiday greeting. Gold edging and embossing add a festive and fun element.

INSPIRATION CORNER

122

*A single Christmas bulb can light up a moment. Ink the holiday light stamp with red and green markers, stamp, then trim, leaving a white edge. Use a glue dot to adhere a loop of gold cord. Stamp a dots square in green ink, then trim leaving a white edge. Glue the green dots on red paper, and then on a white card. Mount the bulb on the green dots using mounting tape.*

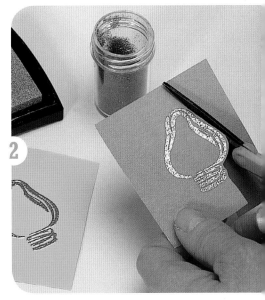

## STEP INSTRUCTION

**ONE** | Edge the deckled area of the card with the red watercolor marker, then edge it with the gold leafing pen. Make a thicker line with the red than the gold, and edge directly over the red with the gold leafing pen.

**TWO** | Stamp the holiday light stamp on the scrap pieces of red, green, blue, yellow and purple cardstock using gold ink. While the ink is still wet on the cardstock, emboss the stamp with gold powder (see page 14 for more information on embossing). When finished and the powder cools, cut out the embossed holiday lights.

**THREE** | Arrange the 12" (30cm) gold cord across the card. Arrange the lights on the cord, turning them in a variety of positions to find a pleasing arrangement. Trim the cord if necessary to keep it from hanging too far over the edge of the card.

**FOUR** | When you're pleased with the arrangement of the lights and cord, adhere the lights to the card with mounting tape. Use the mounting tape under the stamped lights to hold the cord in place.

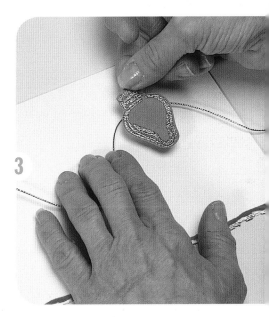

### Tip

When embossing, it's a good idea to stamp with the same colored ink as the embossing powder. The colored ink will help hide imperfections in the embossing.

Materials ◄ 4¼" × 5½" (11cm × 14cm) Deckle-edged ivory card (can be purchased precut and prefolded or see page 71 for information on making your own deckle-edged card) ▸ Red cardstock ▸ Scrap of corrugated brown paper ▸ Holiday swirls and stars stamp (HERO ARTS) ▸ Gold ink ▸ Gold embossing powder ▸ Gold leafing pen ▸ 4" (10cm) Gold cord ▸ Glue stick ▸ Glue dots ▸ 3" (8cm) Circle punch ▸ Scissors ▸ Heat gun

asonal delights cards seasonal delights cards seasonal delights cards seasonal delights card delights cards seasonal delights cards seasonal delights cards seasonal delights cards seaso seasonal delights cards seasonal delights cards seasonal delights cards seasonal delights c light cards seasonal delights cards seasonal delights cards seasonal delights cards seasona asonal delights seasonal delights cards seasonal delights cards seasonal delights card

# Holiday Ornament

THIS HOLIDAY ORNAMENT, DECORATED with embossed swirls and stars, is waiting to adorn a Christmas tree. Attach it to your card for a simple, but beautiful, celebration of the season.

INSPIRATION CORNER

*Everyone loves Christmas trees. Make this simple tree by embossing the swirls stamp twice on green paper. Cut a large triangle from the paper for the tree. Punch out a star from metallic gold paper, and cut a small rectangle from corrugated brown paper for the trunk. Adhere all the pieces on a card.*

## STEP INSTRUCTION

**ONE** | Punch the 3" (8cm) circle out of the red cardstock. Stamp the holiday swirls and stars stamp onto the red cardstock circle using gold ink. The stamp should cover the whole circle, so plan what part of the stamp you will use, and stamp on a protected surface.

**TWO** | While the ink is still wet, use gold embossing powder to emboss the holiday swirls and stars on the red cardstock (see page 14 for more information on embossing).

**THREE** | Cut corrugated paper in a rectangle large enough to fit at the top of the ornament. Ink the ridges of the corrugated paper with the gold leafing pen, giving it gold highlights. Loop the gold cord behind the corrugated paper, holding the loop in place with a glue dot.

**FOUR** | Attach the corrugated paper to the top of the ornament. Secure the bottom edge of the corrugated paper behind the ornament with a glue dot. Use a glue stick to glue the ornament to the center front of the ivory card.

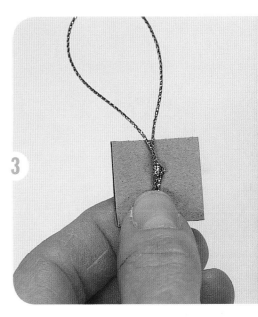

 *Try this!*

Why not make two ornaments for each card? Slip one inside the card for the recipient to use on the tree, and secure the other to the front of the card.

125

# Resources

Most of the supplies used in the book can be found at your local craft, rubber stamping and scrapbook stores. Check the phone book for store locations near you. For help finding a particular product, contact the manufacturers listed below.

## STAMPS

Hanko Designs
(510) 523-5603
www.hankodesigns.com

Hero Arts
(800) 822-4376
www.heroarts.com

Hot Potatoes
(615) 269-8002
www.hotpotatoes.com

Impress
(206) 901-9101
www.impressrubberstamps.com

Mostly Hearts
(866) 789-9874
www.mostlyhearts.com

Posh Impressions
(800) 421-7674
www.poshimpressions.com

Printworks
(800) 854-6558
www.printworkscollection.com

Stampendous
(800) 869-0474
www.stampendous.com

## PAPERS

Crafter's Workshop
(877) 272-3837
www.thecraftersworkshop.com

Design Originals
(800) 877-7820
www.d-originals.com

Hanko Designs
(510) 523-5603
www.hankodesigns.com

Hero Arts
(800) 822-4376
www.heroarts.com

Lasting Impressions
for Paper, Inc.
(800) 9-EMBOSS
www.lastingimpressions.com

Paper Adventures/ANW
(973) 406-5000
www.anwcrestwood.com

Me and My Big Ideas
www.meandmybigideas.com

Metropolis
Paper International
(416) 740-4345
www.metropolispaper.com

Printworks
(800) 854-6558
www.printworkscollection.com

## ADHESIVES

3M
(888) 364-3577
www.3m.com

Glue Dots
(888) 688-7131
www.gluedots.com

Tombow
(800) 835-3232
www.tombowusa.com

## INKS

Clearsnap
(888) 448-4862
www.clearsnap.com

Ranger Industries
(800) 244-2211
www.rangerink.com

Stewart Superior
(800) 621-1205
www.stewartsuperior.com

Tsukineko
(800) 769-6633
www.tsukineko.com

## PUNCHES, EMBELLISHMENTS AND RIBBON

Creative Impressions
(719) 596-4860
www.creativeimpressions.com

EK Success
(800) 524-1349
www.eksuccess.com

May Arts
(203) 637-8366
www.mayarts.com

Midori
(800) 659-3049
www.midoriribbon.com

Posh Impressions
(800) 421-7674
www.poshimpressions.com

Punch Bunch
(254) 791-4209
www.thepunchbunch.com

Uchida of America
(800) 541-5877
www.uchida.com

# Index

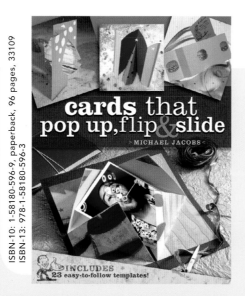

ISBN-10: 1-58180-596-9, paperback, 96 pages, 33109
ISBN-13: 978-1-58180-596-3

ISBN-10: 1-58180-585-3, paperback, 112 pages, 33054
ISBN-13: 978-1-58180-585-7

### CARDS THAT POP-UP, FLIP AND SLIDE | Michael Jacobs

In this creative guide to making dynamic, interactive cards, you'll learn how to craft one-of-a-kind greetings with moving parts such as pop-ups, sliders and flaps. Choose from 22 step-by-step projects that use a variety of papers—from handmade and printed to recycled—to create unique graphic looks. You'll also learn how to create coordinating envelopes to complete the look of your card. You'll be inspired to jazz up all of your cards with the fun and easy techniques in this book, including using inks, collage and colored pencils in fresh new ways.

### STAMPING FUN FOR BEGINNERS | MaryJo McGraw

This is an indispensable, user-friendly handbook for newcomers as well as a great quick-reference guide for seasoned artists. This must-have book features 27 quick and easy projects, like greeting cards, gift tags, boxes, jewelry and journals. It's also filled to the brim with dozens of techniques, including embossing, layering, making your own stamps and more!

ISBN-10: 1-58180-564-0, paperback, 128 pages, 33019
ISBN-13: 978-1-58180-564-2

ISBN-10: 1-58180-746-5, paperback, 96 pages, 33418
ISBN-13: 978-1-58180-746-2

### RETRO MANIA | Judi Watanabe and Alison Eads and Laurie Dewberry

Retro Mania! shows you how to make swell paper-crafts using hot images and graphics from your favorite decades. You'll find 50 projects featuring popular decade-inspired motifs, from the swelle-gant 40s and fabulous 50s to the psychedelic 60s and groovy 70s. You'll love the stylish handmade cards, scrapbook pages and gift ideas. And you might even learn something along the way--the book is packed with fun facts about each era and includes tips on customizing every project to your personal swingin' taste.

### SIMPLY BEAUTIFUL GREETING CARDS | Heidi Boyd

Whether you're a complete beginner or a seasoned crafter, Simply Beautiful Greeting Cards shows you how to create personalized greeting cards for every occasion. You'll find cards that are great for holidays, birthdays, weddings and "just because." With 50 different quick and easy cards to choose from, you'll be eager to show your family and friends how much you care with style and flair. In addition to the wide array of cards, you'll find a helpful section on basic tools and materials as well as a treasure trove of papercrafting tips and tricks.